GOOD KIDS
—WHO DO—
BAD
THINGS

GOOD KIDS
— WHO DO —
BAD
THINGS

JAY STRACK

WORD PUBLISHING
Dallas · London · Vancouver · Melbourne

GOOD KIDS WHO DO BAD THINGS

All Scripture quotations, unless otherwise noted, are taken from The New King James Version (NKJV). Copyright © 1979, 1980, 1982, Thomas Nelson, Inc., Publisher. Verses marked KJV are from The King James Version. PHILLIPS refers to The New Testament in Modern English by J. B. Phillips, published by The Macmillan Company, © 1958, 1960, 1972 by J. B. Phillips.

Library of Congress Cataloging-in-Publication Data

Strack, Jay.
    Good kids who do bad things : how to help your kids make good choices / Jay Strack.
        p.   cm.
    ISBN 0-8499-3398-6
    1. Parent and teenager—United States.   2. Parenting—United States.   3. Parenting—Religious aspects—Christianity.
    I. Title.
HQ799.15.S75   1993
649'.125—dc20   92-46040
                                                                         CIP

3 4 5 9   LB   9 8 7 6 5 4 3 2 1

Printed in the United States of America

Contents

Foreword   7

1   What Is a Good Kid?   9
The Case for Patience and Hope

2   The Lion's Roar   17
It's Dangerous Out There!

3   Beyond the Glitter   33
Kids, Parents, and Popular Culture

4   Fasten Your Seatbelts   43
Getting Ready for the Teenage Years

5   How Do You Spell Problems?   59
Eight Issues Kids Struggle with Most

6   "He's a Rebel"   73
How to Handle Conflict with Your Kids

7   A Matter of Heartitude   83
What Kids Need Most in a Mom
By Diane Strack

8   I'll Climb with You   93
What Kids Need Most in a Dad

9   A Taste of Heaven   105
The Home as God Would Have It

10   Breaking the Cycle of Pain   119
Confronting Family Dysfunctions

11   Friendly Fire   127
Internal Problems That Could Sabotage Your Family

12   Reaching for the Stars   137
How to Motivate Your Kids

13   Get Out the Big Guns   151
The Patriot Missile of Prayer

14   Tearing Down the Chemical Curtain   161
       How to Keep Your Kids from Ever Using Drugs

15   Departed for a Season   175
       Living with (and without) a Prodigal

16   Code Blue   185
       How to Respond When the Going Gets Tough

17   Special Settings   193
       Blended and Single Families

Appendix 1: Stages of Adolescence   199

Appendix 2: Youth Survey Form   203

Notes   205

Foreword

I have never met a "bad kid," but I have met plenty of "good kids" who are prone to do bad things. It's puzzling. What causes a kid who knows right from wrong to turn his back on the values and standards he has been raised to appreciate and abide by? It doesn't make sense—or does it? I believe in most cases that it does.

We live in an evil world. A world committed to the destruction of our integrity, our morality, our marriages, and our kids. Young people today face pressures of such magnitude that even the strongest and most committed among them find themselves blown off course at times. Good kids do bad things because they spend the majority of their time in a society that has become a finely tuned weapon of destruction. A weapon that is targeting their minds, hearts, and bodies.

I agree with Jay, that most of us who are old enough to have children have very little idea of what goes on in the youth culture of our day. We continue to think back to when we were in school. We acknowledge things are worse—but just how much worse, we do not know. But it's time we found out and responded accordingly.

Fortunately, there is hope. In fact, there is a great deal of hope. But it is up to parents to make hope a reality for this generation of kids. The educational system is not the answer. Government programs are not the answer. The family, as God designed it to function, is the answer. The chaos we see around us may have taken us by surprise, but God saw it coming a long time ago and made provision for it. Mom and Dad, you are that provision.

The most powerful force in a child's life is his parents. Jay writes, "Parents are the most crucial factor in the life of a child." Amen!

Why do good kids do bad things? After reading only a few chapters of this book, I believe the fog will begin to clear, the mystery will begin to unfold, and the truth will be evident. In *Good Kids Who Do Bad Things*, Jay Strack offers a clear explanation of the pressures our kids face every day. More importantly, he offers practical, biblical instruction on how parents can work with their children to successfully cope with those pressures.

I thank God for Jay Strack's commitment to young people. Children are indeed a gift from the Lord. *Good Kids Who Do Bad Things* will help you protect this priceless gift.

Dr. Charles F. Stanley
Pastor, First Baptist Church Atlanta

1

What Is a Good Kid?

The Case for Patience and Hope

What is your goal in being a parent?

If you're like most parents, you want to raise "good kids." But what exactly is a good kid, anyway?

I'm quite sure that Amy Carmichael, the bold and courageous missionary to India, would have been evaluated in a treatment center had she pulled some of her childhood shenanigans in the nineties. Elizabeth Elliott says this of Amy:

> The eldest of seven children, she often led the rest of them in wild escapades, such as the time she suggested they all eat laburnum pods. She had been told that the pods were poisonous, and thought it would be fun to see how long it would take them to die.[1]

Was Amy Carmichael a bad child? Her parents didn't think so. Instead, they patiently raised her in the admonition of the Lord. At the age of seventeen, Amy began working with the poor children of Belfast. Eventually she saved the lives of countless Indian children meant to be sold as temple prostitutes and sacrifices.

I took my first drink when I was eight or nine years old. By the time I reached high school, I was not only drinking heavily, but smoking marijuana, popping pills, and taking hallucinogenic drugs. I drove at reckless speeds and took foolish risks. I was arrested four times for drug possession with intent to distribute and for driving under the influence. My fourth arrest came after I got high, plowed my car into a row of taxi cabs, ran away from the scene, and punched an officer. I lost my driver's license and spent months in a juvenile detention center.

Was I a bad kid? A lot of people would probably say so. But there was hope for me, too. One young man took it upon his heart to pray earnestly for me and to share the gospel at every opportunity. Although no one, including myself, ever believed I would do it, I found myself at a Bible study, eagerly hanging on to every word. When an invitation to accept Christ was given, I hopefully accepted. After that, patience, prayer, and caring on the part of family and friends helped me fight the battle of old and new. Today I am a minister with a wonderful calling, a wonderful family, and a special place in my heart for kids in trouble.

A New Definition of Good

So what is a good kid? Maybe it's time to rethink our definition.

To many parents, "good" means good grades, a clean room, no talking back, and, in particular, no embarrassment to the parents. These are certainly desirable qualities, but if we make them our yardstick for good, we may be setting up both ourselves and our kids for heartbreak and disappointment.

Counseling teens and parents in various parts of the country has also shown me that many of us overemphasize outward appearances and whether or not a child or teenager actually "gets caught." In the process, we may ignore the real issues—what's going on inside, and what direction the child is going.

As a result, the girl who makes good grades and is popular may be considered a "good" girl even though she is sexually active. Another girl who becomes pregnant is labeled "bad." Or what of the girl who has an abortion so that her parents may never know about her sexual behavior in comparison to the teen who resolves to deliver the baby and put it up for adoption?

In the same school there may be a football player who works a part-time job, maintains a high average, but drinks every weekend and attempts to "score" with his girlfriend. He is viewed and praised as the "All-American boy." But his classmate with long hair, black clothes, and an earring is categorized as a "problem" child.

Somehow, somewhere, our criteria for grading children as "good" and "bad" have been shaped by society's rules as to what would be embarrassing to a parent or disruptive to a group.

So maybe it's time for a new definition of a good kid. Perhaps it should mean a child who is growing in maturity, who becomes an independent and responsible person. "Good," for me, also means that my children develop an inner strength that enables them to stand alone and resist the stampeding herd of peer pressure. Good kids are those who are growing spiritually, moving closer to God, and learning what it means to live godly lives. Helping our children move in that direction should be our primary goal as parents.

Even Good Kids Choose Wrong

Whatever qualities you feel a child must possess to be good, remember that even good kids can be headed in the wrong direction. Good kids can make bad choices; good kids can do bad things.

Two girls stood after church one night waiting for mom as though they had been there all evening. When asked, "Were you in the service?" they answered yes and even pretended to have heard the special music. But the neighbor who had been doing her grocery shopping that evening told a different story. She had seen the two girls reading magazines in the store during the time of the service.

One young man told his parents he would be at a lock-in all night, but instead he went to a teen nightclub and stayed out all night, dropping by the church in the morning to cover his story.

Either of these incidents, taken alone, might not be a precedent for more trouble by these teens. It depends on whether their parents are smart enough to discover the lies and get to the source of the problem before it can grow.

Solomon wrote of the "little foxes that spoil the vines." For many good kids, it is the unconfessed "small" sins and white lies that bring about an easier transition into "bad." Once the heart begins to harden, once the promptings of the Holy Spirit are ignored, it gets easier and easier to do it over and over again, especially when mom and dad are too blind to catch on. "Do not be deceived, God is not mocked." These children, left to their own deceptions, will reap what they sow.

What Makes a Kid Good?

Many factors will influence your child's future. *Each child is a product of nature, nurture, and the quest to find his or her own niche.* These three factors intertwine to shape the growing child's personality and character.

Nature means the genetic makeup or genetic inheritance—the combination of traits that is unique to the child from the moment of conception. Your child came into this world as a special individual with physical and mental characteristics that can influence behavior and choices. (Ask any parent who raised two easygoing, compliant children and one "firecracker.")

Nature also refers to your child's basic humanity—the traits he or she shares with other humans. The Christian view of humanity is that each of us is an unique creature made in the image of God. We did not originate through a series of accidents, but through the conscious, purposeful, direct handiwork of God. Therefore, every child and adult has a purpose and a reason to be. But the Genesis account reveals that humanity has sinned, and thus is separated from God. The good news is that we are searched for by our loving Creator and heavenly Father. Parents have the privilege and responsibility of helping their children understand this wonderful gift of salvation.

When asked during a "Focus on the Family" broadcast to comment on whether good children are the result of bad experiences or whether good children are born with the tendency toward natural goodness, Dr. James Dobson referred to Psalm 51:5, "in sin my mother conceived me," and to Romans 3:23, "for all have sinned and fall short of the glory of God." "With or without bad experiences," said Dr. Dobson, "a child is naturally inclined toward rebellion, selfishness, dishonesty, aggression, exploitation, and greed. He does not have to be taught these behaviors. They are inevitable expressions of his humanness."

Even secular psychologists and psychiatrists recognize a sense of emptiness and yearning deep within a child. While denying original sin in children, Dr. John Bradshaw, author of *The HomeComing*, recognizes this tendency for rebellion and restlessness and calls it "the metaphysical blues." This built-in restlessness and boredom puts many children and teens on the road to trouble.

Whatever the circumstances, God commands and empowers parents to help their children make the best of life's everyday demands and survive life's unexpected stresses and storms. This is where nurture comes in. Nurture is best described as the care and feeding of the personality through love, security, discipline, and encouragement. Essentially, that's our job as parents. It's also our responsibility to raise our children in the understanding and love of God—to introduce them to the only possible remedy for their natural restlessness and rebellion.

A child's niche will be the result of the many events and circumstances that shape everyone's particular world. From birth, children are influenced by the actions of others. When a child is young, his parents have a tremendous influence. As a child grows, however, many other factors come into play—school, church, society, and peers. But a child's own responses—the decisions he makes and the attitudes he adopts—are equally important in shaping his world.

A Parent's Role

What does this all say about the role of parents? Parents are the most crucial factor in the life of a child. Much of a child's future depends on our willingness to establish a loving, structured environment, to teach our child what he needs to know, and to guide him in making positive decisions. In today's society, a lot depends on our being aware of harmful influences and helping our kids steer a careful course through the possible pitfalls. This book is designed to help you do just that.

But what if it's already too late? What if your good kid is already doing bad things?

First, for your own emotional well-being, learn to spell *relief*. Guilt won't make you a better parent. Besides, the fact that you have picked up this book indicates your concern and places you at the plate ready to take your best swing on behalf of your children.

Even if you've made mistakes in the past, you can make a difference in your kid's future. This is true whether your children are young or if they've already entered the turbulent teenage years. Abraham Lincoln could have had raising children in mind when he said, "The best thing about the future is that it comes one day at a time."

What will it take to help your kids grow in a positive direction?

One strong factor in your favor is love. The strength of an embrace has rescued many a child from the poor hand dealt by nature or neighborhood. Bonds made tough through laughter and struggle stand the test of time. The Johnson family lived in a tough Northeastern ghetto riddled with the trauma of gangs, drug use, and extreme poverty. They were interviewed on radio about the unusual achievements of their children in light of their environment. The children were all drug-free and college graduates. Mrs. Johnson proudly declared, "Hugs protect from drugs, and the only gang allowed around here is the Johnson gang!"

Faith and prayer are absolute essentials in raising good kids. You were never intended to parent your children or live your life on your own strength. It's hard to point your kids toward what they need most—Christ's saving grace—if that grace isn't an important factor in your own life.

Believing in your children is another strong plus. Children will display incorrect and unacceptable behavior, as will adults. Parents must take care to discern the difference between the expression of individuality or exploration of self, on the one hand, and actual "bad" behavior, on the other.

I remember as a child feeling that there were probably going to be two lines at school—one for good kids and the other for bad. At the end of each line I thought they probably rubber-stamped your hand, and that determined what you would be. I didn't remember going through a line, but I felt that every day I was being rubber-stamped "Bad Kid." The truth of "Whatever the mind can believe, it can achieve"—*positively or negatively*—also holds true for children growing up in our homes.

Finally, patience is a must. After all, God knows even our "inward parts," that is, our strengths and our weaknesses (Ps. 139:13), and He is patient about our weaknesses.

John 21 gives a beautiful picture of Jesus' patient approach to our weaknesses—an approach that can be our model in dealing with our children's weaknesses. Peter had forgotten the purpose to which Jesus had called him—to be a fisher of men. Instead he was out in the boat with the boys. Rather than scold Peter, the resurrected Jesus prepared him a meal. In their after-dinner conversation, Jesus forgave Peter for the three times the apostle had denied knowing Him. But even as He pardoned Peter, Jesus required him to answer for his intentions and actions. Twice Jesus asked Peter whether he loved Him with all of his heart. Peter, in his honesty, could not answer yes, but said, "You know that I am Your friend." Although that was not the relationship Jesus wanted from Peter, He was willing to accept that answer because He knew that it was all that Peter could offer at that time. Looking down the road at who Peter would become and what he would accomplish for the cause of Christ, Jesus was willing to receive him as he was, for the moment. No doubt His provision and tolerance spoke volumes to Peter and motivated him to go on and do great things in the name of the Lord. Surely, as he died a martyr's death, Peter could say, "Yes, Lord, You know that I love You with all of my heart."

The old saying, "Please be patient; God isn't finished with me yet!" is a reminder that God never labels us as hopeless. This reality can inspire us to patience and forgiveness as we lead our children to take their sins and mistakes and use them for good. The model of His patient, redeeming love is one we must follow even when our good kids do bad things.

2

The Lion's Roar

It's Dangerous Out There!

The full moon hung shiny as an unspent coin as I stood under the primitive brush arbor and stared out in the dark, unfamiliar jungle. India was a new territory for me. Turning my gaze to my congregation, I smiled to see that children are the same around the world. A group of them sat just a few feet from the platform, their eyes bright and their faces shining with innocence.

But my smile quickly faded as my eye fell on one young girl. Although the left side of her face displayed a pure beauty, the right side was hideously scarred. I knew instantly what had happened. Just a few days earlier, in another village, my heart had lurched with horror over the remains of a young boy who had been ripped apart by an animal of the jungle.

At that moment, as if in response to my thoughts, the darkness was split by a terrifying snarl from the surrounding jungle. Dread and fear spread over the faces around me as the roar of the great jungle beast shattered the wind and shook the thatched arbor . . .

I hear a similar roar today as I examine the clear danger faced by our children as they attempt to walk the treacherous road that leads to adulthood. I am reminded of the "lion" of which the apostle Peter warned so long ago:

> Be sober, be vigilant; because your adversary the devil walks about like a roaring lion, seeking whom he may devour.
>
> 1 Peter 5:8

Since that day in the jungle many years ago, I have spoken to scores of teenagers whose lives have been ripped apart or scarred by their adversary, "the roaring lion." Those memories are vividly imprinted in my mind, and I constantly feel the need to warn parents and children that Satan stalks his prey—watching, waiting for the opportunity to pounce.

The word Peter uses for *adversary* is an old word for an opponent in a lawsuit. Parents must never forget that this enemy will slander and accuse them in the eyes of their own children in an attempt to coerce teens to run ahead or fall behind the protection and care of their families. Satan attacks on all sides, threatening body and soul, mind and spirit. His attacks have perhaps never been fiercer than in our present age.

In a real sense, today's parents are fighting a fierce battle for their children. As I see it, the battle is raging in three arenas. First is the battle for the mind, which involves the constant assault of anti-Christian values. Second is the battle for the body, which primarily involves sexual sin. Third is the battle for the family, which involves the breakup of homes. Let's take a look at these battlegrounds and point out the weapons provided to us by He who empowers us in the fight.

The Battle for the Mind

Peter alerts us to the battle for the mind with these urgent words: "Be sober." The word *sober* literally means to have a sound and healthy mind, to guard and protect our thoughts. The word picture is that of building a defensive wall around the mind—like the massive walls that used to protect cities from invaders.

The Scripture makes it clear that our children's thoughts determine the direction of their lives: "As he thinks in his heart, so is he" (Prov. 23:7). Since Satan knows this, he daily assaults the hearts and minds of our children with the battering rams of anti-Christian values.

Some of these are even advocated in the schools. The media bombard children with images designed to seduce them from the teachings of Scripture and common decency. The fruit basket of values offered children by schools, media, and home is then mixed together and offered again by their peers. Unfortunately, the values of their peers, who serve as a kind of surrogate parent in the lives of many young people today, often win out over those of their parents and their church.

What messages are our children getting? A thorough examination of the value choices confronting our homes reveals a conflict of visions. The world offers visions of a limited importance and a limited future, which I believe produce a vision of a limited life. Here are just a few of the visions the world is offering our kids:

"Humans Are Just Highly Evolved Animals"

Many educators and parents are concerned that, in the name of science, we are chiseling away at the foundation of our children's self-esteem by propagating the unproven theory of evolution. What a child believes about his origin shapes his belief about his destiny. What she believes about her Creator will determine her respect for the Creator's laws. We need to teach our children the truth about the origin of the world and of life.

The Bible teaches us that we have value and worth because we are made in the image of God. Yet the impact of evolutionary thought on several generations of Americans has been to devalue human life. If we believe that humans began as specks of matter in a salty pond millions of years ago, as the advocates of evolutionary theory want us to believe, then humanity is no more noble than, as one philosopher put it, a swarm of mosquitoes.

Evolution is an admitted guess, a theory; it has never been proved as scientific fact. An enormous amount of scientific evidence backs up the claims of Scripture. Humans are biologically distinct from animals in blood, in bone, in flesh, in cells, in mind, in soul, and in spirit. Evolutionary theory offers no explanation for the origin of the first cell. It would be a greater miracle to have the world as we know it evolve from a single speck of protoplasm or from an explosion of gases than from the kind of orderly creation the Bible describes.

There are really only two options, and both require faith. One must choose either the explanation found in Genesis—that humanity is a supernatural creation—or the evolutionary theory that humans are the product of a mechanistic and impersonal universe.

"You're Going to Have Sex—So Do It Safely"

Many of us have heard for years that two things are certain—death and taxes. As a parent, you can surely add a third: someone, somewhere is going to teach your child about sex—whether it is Johnny-know-it-all down the street, a cable show that comes "accidentally" through to your television while you're away one evening, or a class at school.

Most pulpits stress that the home is the place where sex education must be taught, where values are to be instilled, where moral decisions are to be made. Statistics, however, indicate that parents as a whole have abdicated their responsibility, leaving society—including the public schools—to take it on themselves. Unfortunately, the results have been disastrous.

I agree with Tim LaHaye when he says, "Teaching sex education in mixed classes to hot-blooded teenagers without the benefit of biblical or moral values is like pouring gasoline on emotional fires. An explosion is inevitable."[1]

Offering explicit and graphic sex education without moral values is worse than not teaching it at all. It leads to experimentation with very little restraint and is a definite infringement of the family's right and responsibility to teach decisions based on Scripture.

The teachers' motivation is not in doubt or question, but whether they can or should communicate someone else's moral values. The child in the classroom hears a conflicting message to the teaching of mom and dad that sex outside of marriage is wrong. Suddenly, this authority figure, the teacher, very casually discusses sexual intercourse in a room full of male and female peers. When the teacher says, "Sixty-five percent of you are sexually active," whether *implied* or not, the child wonders, *Am I the only virgin in the class?*

Any fears about sex are swiftly dispelled and any facts that may be lacking because of inexperience are supplied and explained in careful detail—while at the same time the class is taught about safety through condoms. Now the child thinks, *Can there be any risk of pregnancy or disease if I use a condom the way the teacher is showing me? It can't be so bad if the teacher is explaining how.*

Of course, school boards defend themselves with statistics, particularly those regarding teenage pregnancies and AIDS and HIV. The national average seems to be that more than 50 percent of today's teenagers are sexually active; in many schools the figure is more than 75 percent. They're going to do it anyway, the schools say, so we need to give them proper information. But *are* they going to do it anyway? Statistics show an alarming parallel between the escalation of sexual promiscuity and the increased amount of more in-depth sex education.

The school system in the industrial community of Commerce City, Colorado, was one of the first in the nation to hand out condoms. In the spring of 1991, three years later, the birthrate among high school girls in Commerce City was *31 percent* above the national average. In 1991, seventy-six students in Commerce City became teen mothers, and more than a hundred were expected in 1992.[2]

This "progressive" school system has had a teen parenting program since 1979. But some people, including many students, think this just glorifies having a baby. They argue that the nursery set up on campus tempts vulnerable girls by putting the cute and cuddly babies on display. Having a baby, they believe, has become a status symbol.[3]

Still the school boards cry out for more "sex education." On a daily basis, the average teen is bombarded inside the classroom and out with sexual information. The crude graffiti on bathroom walls is but another form of the neatly printed literature given out by counselors and teachers. While we say no to R-rated movies and MTV, our children are watching videos in the classroom that would make most parents blush.

It would seem to be an excellent idea to put at least as much time, energy, and hope in God's plan for His creation as in this process of trying to make teens wiser. Knowledge without wisdom results in emptiness.

Even Dr. Benjamin Spock says that the best precautions against AIDS "are education and a belief that the spiritual aspects of love are as important as the purely physical. The surest way to avoid AIDS, of course, is to delay intercourse until marriage."[4]

The bottom line is that you can have the greatest impact on your child's sexual choices and behaviors. It is one giant step toward winning the battle for the mind.

"Drink Responsibly"

Drinking has long been glamorized by attractive (and expensive) advertising. Sex, humor, sports, and celebrities are used to push the product. The tragedy of these slick and enticing advertisements is that children are becoming more and more aware of and attracted to alcohol at younger ages.

In a survey of more than a half-million school-age children, the popular educational newspaper *Weekly Reader* found that 34 percent of fourth graders felt "some" or "a lot" of pressure to try wine coolers or beer. According to figures from the National Council on Alcoholism, the average age of those starting to use alcohol is twelve.

Perhaps the most dangerous promotion has been the covert emphasis adopted by some school systems of drinking "responsibly." As I speak in middle schools and high schools across this nation, I am often dismayed over the number of posters proclaiming "Don't drink and drive" or "Know when to say when." You may have seen the poster with the caption, "You're old enough to drink, but are you mature enough to drink?" How many teens would really reply, "Oh, well, I guess I'm not mature enough"?

Drinking responsibly is actually a gross contradiction of terms, particularly for teenagers. The *Journal of the American Medical Association* cited a scientific study of 11,631 students, grades nine through twelve from all fifty states, reporting that 54 percent acknowledged occasional use of alcohol. More than 35 percent admitted to alcoholic binging. What makes these statistics even more tragic and frightening is that teenage bodies are three times more susceptible to alcohol addiction than adult bodies. For this reason, many young people become alcoholics within six months of their first drink.[5]

To be completely honest, though, commercials and misdirected educational emphasis are not nearly as influential on these young people as is the behavior of their own parents. The mere fact that some form of alcohol is present in 70 percent of American homes is a temptation too great for many teens. When we drink, we teach our children that this powerful liquid can cure what ails you and that drinking is an adult thing to do. Is it any wonder that teenagers are drawn to it?

The Battle for the Body

No matter how many times I speak in schools or how many teens I talk to, I can never get used to the empty look of a young girl who comes to me "in trouble." I can see even before she approaches me that the glow of innocence is gone and that the carefree life of a child has ended. She has lost a major skirmish in the battle for the body, the pressure toward sexual sin.

Perhaps Peter was speaking from personal experience in the passage with which we began this chapter; the next word picture he paints is that we should "Be vigilant" (1 Pet. 5:8). The Greek term means "to be alert" and "to watch your step." In the original grammatical construction, both warnings are in the active verb form. "Be sober" means to be mentally alert. "Be vigilant" means to be morally alert, to guard and protect our children and to equip them to win the battle for the body.

Teens At Risk

Which teens are most at risk to lose the battle for the body? First, teens who drink or use drugs are very susceptible to impulsive decision making, which often results in sexual intercourse. A young man or young woman who is high or drunk will have lower inhibitions and often heightened sexual awareness—a dangerous combination. Every nightclub and bar offers at least one "ladies' night" during the week when women can enter and/or drink free. The owners know that this scheme will draw three or four times as many men, attracted by the very real possibility that women who have had too much to drink might be easily seduced.

Another group that is very vulnerable is made up of those who are allowed too much freedom at too young an age. Numerous surveys and studies have revealed the risk that latchkey kids face on a daily basis. Even though the child might be reporting in to mom, he may only be reporting part of the truth.

One night after I had preached on "Sex, Love, and Dating," Jeff came to me to share his story. Every day after school he would come home to an empty house and dutifully call his mother at work. "I love you, Mom," he would say. "I just wanted to let you know that I'm home. What time do you think you'll be in so I can start supper for you?" Mom was so proud of her son and so sure of his maturity, she never questioned him. Yet every afternoon Jeff brought his girlfriend to the house where they would have sexual intercourse after he had checked in with mom to make sure she wouldn't walk in unannounced.

After several months, Jeff began to notice that he wasn't feeling up to par. He checked with the school nurse and discovered that his girlfriend had given him a sexually transmitted disease which required long-term treatment. He had to tell his mom the whole truth. She was shocked, having never believed that her polite son could be so deceptive. He simply wasn't ready for that much freedom.

When most of today's parents were growing up, the danger of going "too far" usually occurred in the back seat of a car while "parking." Today it is not uncommon at all for teens to have sex in their own beds in their own homes. When *Seventeen* magazine asked, "For those of you who've had sex, where are you having it?" the answers were as follows:

	Girls	Boys
Partner's house/bedroom	78%	65%
Own house/bedroom	78%	72%
Hotel/motel	40%	31%
At a party	22%	35%

(Total exceeds 100% due to multiple mentions.)

Other answers given were outdoors, such as a park or the woods, and someone else's house.

One columnist ran an article from a shocked woman whose neighbor had called her to arrange a sexual liaison between her daughter and the neighbor's son. She explained that since this was the age of sexual peak for her son (according to studies), she wanted to make sure that he was with partners who were using birth control and who were disease free. She was calling the mothers of friends to make up an available "list" for the boy and wanted her permission before going ahead.

These teens are being asked to shoulder emotions that they simply are not able to handle. In later years when they fall in love in a monogamous relationship, it will be difficult to understand the beauty and intimacy of the sexual relationship in marriage. God's intention of sexuality as a sacred trust has been mutilated into a fun pastime. These young people are set up for a lifetime of never having enough and permanent emotional scarring.

The Role of Role Models

Although the role models available to our children are varied, the celebrities with the most visibility are often the ones portraying the wrong message. Elizabeth Wyatt, professor of medical psychology at UCLA, says that girls latch onto provocative entertainers like Madonna as role models and end up "playing a stereotypical role of a highly sophisticated woman. And below that is a confused and lonely youngster seeking approval."[6]

Biography after biography boasts of sexual conquests in great numbers. Wilt Chamberlain, a hero to many young boys, brags about being with twenty thousand different women. Geraldo Rivera named so many celebrities with whom he supposedly slept that it made the talk show and magazine circuit for months. Perhaps even more disturbing is the way that disc jockeys in many major markets have given these purported conquests much attention and exposure during prime-time listening hours.

My greatest fear is that many young men are growing up in abusive homes or single-parent homes where they never really see the way God intended for a man to treat a woman. As a young boy, it was not uncommon for me to see my stepfather slap my mother and come home drunk after having been out with another woman. As a teenager, it was not uncommon for the men who came and went in my life to ridicule and belittle me if I was not sexually active. For many years I believed this was acceptable, if not normal, behavior for a man. Add to this the constant bombardment of the songs and videos that glamorize women as victims, and we see little chance for women to be respected in the present or the future.

When Innocence Ends

After having spent these last twenty years speaking to teenagers about this battle for the body, I would like to offer several observations about what happens when the battle is lost and innocence is ended.

First, the younger a girl is when she becomes sexually active, statistically, the greater the likelihood that she will end up a pregnant teenager and/or sexually involved with multiple partners. The chance that she will find what she really wants—love—is almost nil.

If she does become pregnant, the "easy" answer seems to be abortion. A growing number of parents, even in the church, are insisting on abortions, even over the objection of the teen herself. It doesn't really matter, though, whether mom wants it or not—in some states, a teenage girl can have an abortion and be back home before mom ever knows anything about it. *USA Today* computed in January 1989 that the chances of being killed by terrorists overseas were 1 in 50,000 while the chance of being killed in the womb of an American woman is 1 in 3.3. Abortion is becoming just that common.

One girl told me she raised the money for an abortion from friends, and she thought it would be so easy. But now, months later, the guilt was eating her alive. Deceiving her parents, violating her own beliefs, and altering her young body were all more than she could bear. In desperation, she began to run from herself by taking hard drugs and running with a party-hardy crowd. She began giving herself away sexually to various young men in an effort to prove that sex was just a fun game with no emotions or strings. Her goal was to burn herself out in mind and body in order to erase the pain. The end of innocence should not have to hurt so much.

Second, young men are increasingly exposed to pornography, not only in hard-core magazines or adult book stores, but also the "soft porn" of various cable programs, the constant sexual content of MTV videos, and movies. J. Allan Peterson summarizes this process that takes one from lustful thought to illicit action like this: "Our minds feed the fantasy, the fantasy creates the emotions, and the emotions scream for the actual experience."[7]

It is not uncommon for a young lady to come to me after an assembly with tears as she confesses, "I didn't want to have sex until I was married, but I've been so lonely and he made me feel so loved and cared for." As a parent, you must understand that often a young lady will use sex in order to get love, but a young man will often use, "I love you," in order to get sex. Being surrounded by people is not an automatic cure for loneliness.

The young man who is struggling with his small stature or underdeveloped body will look to celebrities and rock stars as models—stars who are famous but may not be morally impressive. What they see and hear is the "ladies man" bragging about sex. The young lady who feels like an ugly duckling may try to learn flirtation techniques or use suggestive language to gain entrance into a group. *When 50 to 75 percent of their peers are involved in sexual activity, it may begin to seem "common" to our children.*

It is up to us to reinforce consistently the plan of God for safe sex and healthy emotions—abstinence until marriage. Don't overdo it by making a big deal out of "The Talk," or by giving them more than they are ready for. Don't pry. Never accuse. Talking is a good place to start, but we must *enable* our children to deal with their sexuality in godly fashion through constant emotional and prayerful support. The goal is to guide our children into adopting the standard of Scripture as their own personal standard. Then it is no longer mom and dad's conviction; it is now *my* conviction.

The apostle Peter's warning that Satan, as a roaring lion, seeks our destruction is ironic, in that the leading causes of destruction among young people are also the leading causes of divorce.

The Battle Against Breaking Up

The question asked most by children and young people today is: "Mom and Dad, do you still love each other?" It's a question that is on the minds of the children of even the closest families. The day has come when the divorce court gavel is pounding so loudly and so quickly that the wedding bells cannot be heard. The noise is not only destroying the relationship between husbands and wives; it is destroying youth as well.

I will always remember the day my daughter Christina came home devastated by the news: "My friend's daddy left her." Her tears were tears of sympathy for the little girl and for the mother, a teacher at her Christian school and a lovely woman outside as well as inside.

As I listened to my daughter's story and wiped away her tears, she looked into my eyes and asked, "Daddy, you won't ever divorce us, I mean, Mom, will you?"

At first I was hurt that my daughter could ask such a question of me. But then I understood. It was not the atmosphere of our home that gave her doubts; it was the tremors of falling homes all around her that caused her insecurity. "Of course not, Honey," I replied. My wife Diane and I joined hands together as a sign of our love and told Christina of our pledge of commitment to each other and to our children. Using my best "rap" voice, I responded, "We're too legit to quit!"

All around them, our children see homes crashing and marriages dissolving. Their whole concept of being accepted unconditionally by parents and by others can be shattered when they believe that mom and dad can stop loving each other. *After all, they are thinking, what promise do I have that dad won't stop loving me? How do I know that mom won't decide it's not worth the worry and work?*

By the time they are in their teens, young people are showing signs of maturity, or at least attempting to. So it is often thought that they can cope with divorce more easily than younger children. In fact, the opposite may be true. Teens are already full of insecurity. They are searching for identity. A deep sense of abandonment at this point in their lives can result in a lack of trust in other emotional relationships.

Because teenagers tend to act out their sense of rejection and abandonment, their response to divorce is often destructive. They have access to automobiles, drugs, and alcohol. It is not uncommon at all for a girl or boy to decide to try sex at this time in an attempt to reestablish security, love, and intimacy. The fractured family is a compounded burden to their tumultuous passage through adolescence.

We see in Genesis that the first attack on the family came when Adam and Eve were apart from each other. Perhaps if they had been together when Satan confronted them, their united strength would have enabled them to withstand temptation, making possible a different ending to the story.

The lion roars at the family in hopes of separating the young from the protection of the parents through the decision to divorce.

The Battle Against Losing Heart

Parenting is hard work, a labor of love. It is not the place for those with cold feet or the faint of heart. Many choose to give up in frustration, while still more muddle along with no purpose, hoping that everything will work itself out eventually. Still other parents lose their zest for each other, which always affects their enthusiasm for the hard work of parenting, too.

The wise man counseled, "Keep your heart with all diligence, for out of it spring the issues of life" (Prov. 4:23). Sometimes mom and dad are careless about protecting the heart of their marriages. Too many couples no longer look forward to intimate, heartfelt issues such as being alone together. Their conversations become shallow, little annoyances go unmentioned, and sexual excitement has faded. Marriage is now a routine. Even though the marriage may seem stable to outsiders, the married couple has allowed endurance to replace enjoyment in the marriage.

The Vision in Your Bones

Where can parents find the motivation to keep on trying, to keep their families together despite discouragement, frustration, or even boredom? I believe we need the burning call of parenthood that God can put in our hearts if we open ourselves to His standards, His guidance, and His help.

Nehemiah had this kind if fiery inner vision in his bones as he rebuilt the walls of Jerusalem. When two enemy leaders asked him to come down and talk things over, Nehemiah replied: "I am doing a great work, so that I cannot come down" (Neh. 6:3).

Two elements of this story give us the keys to staying motivated as parents. First, Nehemiah believed with all of his heart and soul that this work was a *great* task. It required all his commitment, his vision, his tenacity, and his leadership. Before parents can enjoy the work of raising children, they must believe that this work of parenting is a great calling. It is not a side business, not an experimental venture, and not a natural evolutionary process. *Our attitude must be that parenting is the most significant endeavor of our lives because it is the high calling of God.*

Second, Nehemiah told his enemies in no uncertain terms, even after the fourth plea, "*I cannot come down.*" He was letting them know that no diversion they could present could cause him to lower his standard or to cease his work, even temporarily. Many of the best intentions of parents have fallen to diversions and discouragement. As long as there is any thought of giving up, the temptation to give up will gain strength.

The exchange of control in the home from parent to child occurs when the parent voluntarily relinquishes it by giving in to depression. If Nehemiah had measured his work daily and evaluated the difficulties, or even the "impossibility" of the task at hand, he would quite likely have quit. I believe that what kept him going was a blazing vision of the completed wall that he kept securely tucked into his memory.

We must not become discouraged and lose heart simply because our efforts at parenting do not always show immediate results. You cannot judge the child today as a finished product, nor can you decide the outcome based on the many obstacles needing to be overcome. *The goal of parents is not to make the child but to enable him or her.* No matter how fiercely the lion roars, we must not lose heart.

3

Beyond the Glitter

Kids, Parents, and Popular Culture

The advertising industry specializes in spreading glitter on anything and everything. It is estimated that the average American is exposed to fifteen hundred commercial messages each day.[1] Growing teenagers are mesmerized by the glitter of the famous, the glamorous, the dynamic, and the attractive—especially the stars in the music and entertainment industry. Product makers from jean companies to vitamins know that celebrities sell.

Every day young people turn to their teen idols to see how to dress, what to say, and how to wear their hair. Adopting a popular image is safe and gives an instant sense of security. As parents, we must work hard at exposing the true nature and character behind the glittery lifestyle.

In our home, instead of ignoring this adoration, I have chosen to be involved in my girls' perception of the popular culture around them. Whenever I have the opportunity, we discuss the facts, good and bad, about the people they admire. I try to get them to discuss role models by asking questions like, "Why would you or wouldn't you adopt this behavior or lifestyle?"

Recently the girls videotaped a popular music awards program so we could watch it together later. Now, I am not the least bit interested in these awards or in the stars, but my daughters are; so we watched and we talked.

Wearing a robe embroidered with a body-sized cross, two well-known performers opened the show with a gospel duet. The song gave thanks for salvation, for love, for a personal God. Then, almost without exception, every person and group accepting an award began by thanking the Lord. They addressed Him as "the High One," "Almighty God," or with some other seemingly "reverential" term.

The next day, the newspaper reported that one group in particular had to be asked to tape over profane words they proudly wore on their jackets. This group's leader was one who thanked the Lord at the beginning of his speech.

While we watched the show, one of my girls would say, "Why, they must be Christians!" But as it continued she soon understood that for many of the entertainers those words were from the mouth and not the heart. We discussed the dress styles (some of it very revealing), the content of their conversation, the kind of music they sang, and compared all this with what the Bible says about the marks of a Christian. Using discussion rather than lecturing, I was very careful not to imply a spirit of self-righteous judgment, but one of careful discernment for all our sakes, not just for theirs.

Hollywood's Strategy

Perhaps the most pervasive and influential medium today is the film industry. Teens are devoted to their films, whether in the cinema or at the video store. (In 1987, income from video rental and sales was nearly twice as much as that of the theaters. That year movie rentals netted $4.4 billion.)

One of the most provocative and informative books that I have ever read on the battle for the mind is called *Dancing in the Dark*. Written by a team of scholars from Calvin College led by Quentin Schultze, it traces the evolution of Hollywood's strategy, beginning in the late sixties and early seventies. The basic ideas are:

1. A younger child will watch anything that an older one will watch.
2. An older child will not watch anything a younger child will watch.

3. A girl will watch anything a boy will watch.

4. A boy will not watch anything that a girl will watch.

5. In order to catch the biggest audience, the film must focus on nineteen-year-old males.

As the seventies moved into the eighties, production companies became experts at getting the teen audience. As one screenwriter put it, it's easier to appeal to teens, "because you don't need a Redford. You need a bunch of kids, girls in tight jeans with ample breasts, and some sort of thin thread of a story."[2]

Now, in the nineties, many parents are deeply disturbed by the vulgarity, violence, and sexual titillation in many films. Objections to these movies have come from many corners, not only conservative and religious. Feminist groups complain of violence toward women, and minorities vent their concern that they are patronized in modern movies. Psychiatrist Thomas Radecki of the National Coalition on Television Violence argues that there is sufficient statistical evidence to link 25 to 50 percent of contemporary social violence to violent entertainment.[3]

The authors of *Dancing in the Dark* say this about the sexual content of current films:

> Sex is almost always a principal subject, represented as a teenage obsession and, more often than not, the primary source of teenage identity. Teen films exalt sex, picturing it as the chief goal and the pinnacle of human experience. According to these films, sex is the best toy in the playpen of adolescence. The only genuine tragedy is chastity, or worse than that, virginity. The sexual act itself is romanticized and can supposedly transform a young person's life. Within the world of teen film, then, sex becomes a panacea.[4]

This is accomplished with no regard to unwanted pregnancy, sexually transmitted diseases, or social or emotional anguish. Once again, our teens are blinded by the glitter.

If you are wondering whether teens are thinking about having sex, all you have to do is turn on almost any sitcom dealing with teenagers to find that at some point in the show the star or stars will deal with this decision. Unfortunately, the decision is discussed with an adult who asks, "Do you think you are ready for this emotionally?" Over 95 percent of the sex broadcast through the media into the homes of America give the impression that sex is the most important, fun-filled, no-risk activity of those in the know. Television is now a new version of the sex education classroom.

It is a fact that sex sells—blue jeans, perfume, soft drinks, and almost anything. On more than one occasion I can remember my daughter asking, "What exactly were they selling in that commercial?" One jean company ran television ads in which one teenager asked another, "Do you ever wonder about your parents having sex?" What does that have to do with jeans?

What disturbs me most are the suggestive commercials that come on during the family sitcom hour. In between funny households and G-rated comedy, families are exposed to commercial after commercial of an adult series that is to follow. It leaves a teen wondering, *What am I missing?* I have no hesitation in asking my daughter to turn the television off or change the channel during these PG-13 types of commercials. In fact, many times I don't even have to ask.

Whether television imitates life or life imitates television is unclear, but a glance at the television section of the Sunday paper gives some perspective on the nature of the tremors in homes today. Most of the prime-time sitcoms are stories of a single dad or mom or a blended family. For years one rarely saw a traditional family presented as "normal." It was refreshing at last to note the popularity of the new family programming which has been spawned by the success of "The Cosby Show"—but its influence may be ended soon.

Because of the effect of the media, children are being hurried along into adult situations. Role models we cannot control portray damaging behavior as so much fun and degenerate lifestyles as so much larger than life. Because youthful eyes are often blinded by the glitter of the world, we must be on the lookout daily for the tracks that betray the lion's presence long before we hear his deafening roar. The church, the home, and the school must work hand in hand to strip away the glitter and reveal the true dangers in the media images presented to the minds of teens.

Don't Just Say No

Don't make the mistake of saying no before you are fully informed, or of prohibiting without enabling your child to understand your point. It's not a question of your authority; it's an opportunity to make a stand based on moral values and Scripture. One of the great commandments for parents is, "Thou shalt not prohibit without providing an alternative and an explanation." "Because I said so!" just won't cut it.

Onc reason for an ongoing gathering of information is *change*. The closer your children come to the ages of ten and above, the more prepared both of you need to be for change. Change can be very frightening for the child *and* the parent! Some children climb the mountain without ever slipping or falling. Others are afraid of the heights. Then there are those who actually slide or fall and need assistance in getting back up to begin climbing again.

If you find that these rapid changes are causing you to say no more and more, beware. A constant no sets up two situations. First, it feeds curiosity. Not only did curiosity kill the cat; it has done in many a teenager. Second, it sends a signal that says "Don't ask any more." So the teen just sneaks around to learn what he can instead of communicating his curiosity to the parent.

For example saying no to all secular music leaves a major vacuum and an impossible rule for your child. Rock music is everywhere—the grocery store, the dentist's office, the mall, and even some churches. Instead, discuss the criteria for acceptable and unacceptable music. Give teens a chance to define guidelines and be part of the decision. They must be guided to make their own determination rather than only accepting yours.

A Joint Research Project

I noticed that as my children were approaching their teen years their curiosity about celebrities and rock stars began to escalate. Since my interest in these idols was minimal, I found that I had to educate myself in order to educate them. I asked them to list the ones they were most interested in. Then I began to collect newspaper and magazine articles about these various personalities, and we read them together.

We discussed how they felt about each star, and whether they agreed or disagreed with their behavior and mode of dress. Even as preteens they were able to tell me their defin :e feelings and why. Where they were unsure, we used biblical principles to decide. I also found that their total infatuation could turn to utter revulsion in a matter of days!

Perhaps as a parent you are not aware that you can go into many music stores and ask to see the cassette or CD insert of a particular album. Often they have one open and will be happy to share it with you. Look inside for the words to the songs. Read them over carefully, making mental notes. Also look over the insert for suggestive photos or questionable language. By doing this, my daughters and I have made intelligent decisions about buying or not buying an album. Many times I find that it is clean, fun music that we can agree on. When I find it unsuitable, I at least am able to share why, and then we make the decision together.

I know that as teens get older it will be harder to have this control. That is why informed choices must become a habit early on and then be adopted into their own thinking. It goes back to the freedom of choosing moral excellence.

Criteria for Teen Music

Even though we may agree on some music and movie selections, I still feel that time limits must be set. Whatever the mind is filled with will begin to mold the person.

In addition to the sheer quantity of time teens spend listening to music, we use a threefold test in examining music: the *music* itself, the *message* of the song, and the *messengers* of the music.

Elements of Music

All music is derived from three basic elements: melody, harmony, and rhythm. These basic elements cannot be considered either evil or good. The way these elements interrelate, as well as the instrumentation used, results in the varied forms and styles of music, including today's rock music. Because music affects emotions, the lyrical content and presentation are important.

Remember that Satan himself was created to be an instrument of praise. Ezekiel 28 informs us that he was an angel created to glorify God through praise and music (v. 13). In the Bible, music is used to praise, worship, and glorify the Lord. But Satan, as the prince of the power of the air, uses music to cast down, to discourage, and to blaspheme.

The Message

So many times teens sing along with songs and buy albums when they do not realize what they are singing. Even if they know some of the words, it is important to evaluate the whole message of the song. We cannot be careless in entertaining thoughts and phrases that deal with suicide, sexual promiscuity, drugs, or Satan worship. When determining what the music were offering, ask, "What would happen if the advice of the song were taken?"

The Messenger

Look with caution at the figure being set up as a hero. Teach your teen that popularity, success, wealth, and even beauty will fade away. Be aware of the lifestyles and the morality stands of these stars. A man or woman who advocates sex before marriage, homosexuality, or drug use ought not to be admired by a Christian.

When Michael Jackson's "Dangerous" video came out in early 1992, the media hype seemed to saturate the conversations at school and among teens as they speculated about his comeback.

I knew that if I did not sit down with my children to watch this video and discuss it afterward, their curiosity would have them searching for it outside of our home and our influence.

My wife and I previewed the much-hyped video and decided that we wanted our children to see it as a help in learning to discern for themselves, since they will be bombarded for the rest of their lives with the enticements and glitter of the entertainment industry. At the conclusion of the joint viewing, I asked them these questions:

1. What is there about the video that you feel is objectionable?

2. Does this directly violate any particular Christian principle?

3. Does the video contain any positive or profitable ideas or theme?

I quickly discovered that the girls shared the same concerns and objections that I did. It was also very gratifying to discuss the public outcry about the offensive portions of the video, and Jackson's decision to edit these out. We talked about making a difference by voicing our beliefs and making a stand.

Help for Evaluating Media

I want to recommend a remarkable publication that our girls are excited about. Focus on the Family publishes two magazines for teens—*Brio* (for girls) and *Breakaway* (for boys). Popular teen idols in music, movies, television, and sports are interviewed and featured. The strong Christian standards of each one leaves an excellent positive image in the mind of my girls as they read of personal struggles, triumphs, and decisions. In addition, the magazines feature a write-in column that openly and honestly discusses current music videos and albums from rap to country and everything in between, and television shows and stars. It presents factual information and leaves teens able to make their own decisions based on Christian principles and morals.

One of the most common trespasses teens commit against parents is sneaking into R-rated movies. The rating system as designed by the secular movie industry is like playing "Let's Make a Deal"—you never know what's behind door number one! I strongly recommend that you do your homework.

An excellent place to start is the *Morality in Media* newsletter published in Dallas. Here movies are reviewed before they are released to the public and are rated according to types of language used, violence, sexual suggestion and/or scenes, drug use, and other offensive situations. In addition, a brief synopsis of the plot is given. *Morality in Media* also publishes a family video guide, recommending more than eight hundred movies that are based on traditional family values.

You should make a point to review personally music and entertainment labeled "parental guidance." Obviously, I am not proposing or endorsing looking at pornography, R-rated movies, or other obviously unsuitable materials. I am just saying that no publication can make the final decision for you. I discovered that my opinions can be wrong if they were based on rumor or inaccurate information. I've learned the hard way that I must do my homework to earn and maintain credibility with my children.

Finally, I want to stress again the rule, "Don't prohibit without providing an alternative." You only set an opportunity for deception by tempting children beyond their ability to bear. There are so many quality movies that are interesting and even fun. There is so much wonderful contemporary Christian music from light to heavy rock, country and western, rap, secular, and everything in between. Introduce this kind of quality as a way of life to your children as they are growing up, and their enjoyment of and agreement on good entertainment will follow naturally.

4

Fasten Your Seatbelts

Getting Ready for the Teenage Years

The Bermuda Triangle is a section of the Atlantic Ocean in which more than fifty ships and twenty planes have mysteriously disappeared. Records of unexplained mishaps in the area date back to the mid-nineteenth century. The legend was revived recently with the discovery of several planes on the ocean floor that might have been the five planes lost in 1945 from the Fort Lauderdale Naval Air Station on a routine training flight. Before contact faded out, they radioed for navigational assistance. A subsequent rescue mission also vanished without a trace. No explanation or acceptable theory has ever been established for the mystery of the Bermuda Triangle.

Returning from an idyllic vacation in Bermuda, I leaned over to my wife and lovingly said, "Honey, we've just entered the Bermuda Triangle!" Then I began humming the theme from "The Twilight Zone." Her immediate reflex action was an elbow into my ribs.

Just as quickly as Diane responded to my joke, the plane also seemed to respond. Suddenly it dropped a few hundred feet, throwing food and trays into the air and dropping oxygen masks into our faces. The panic, however brief, was indeed real. A plane full of frightened people then heard the captain announce with an official sounding voice, "Ladies and gentlemen, please notice that the 'Fasten Seatbelt' sign has been turned on as we are anticipating turbulence ahead." His instructions to prepare for a rough ride, although correct, were a bit tardy!

As your children approach the mysterious phenomenon known as adolescence, the Scripture announces, "Fasten your seatbelt and prepare for turbulence." The loss of communication may at times seem like your children have indeed lost contact with the tower.

If we were to gather together all the passages of Scripture dealing with parenting and the family, we would find that the one common thread of instruction is to *prepare*. The Bible emphasizes the need for parents to prepare themselves and their children for the teenage years to ensure a safe arrival on the mainland of adulthood.

The value of the word *prepare* comes into focus even more clearly when we understand its Latin origin. This all-inclusive word comes from the Latin *paro*. It means "to point in the right direction," "to equip for battle," or "to make complete."

To Point in the Right Direction

We are all born as originals, but eventually we become carbon copies. If you examine your own life, you will agree that you have, at least at some time, patterned or copied your appearance and style from someone else. Thus, we should not be surprised when our children begin to do so. We should constantly remind ourselves that our children have been "created in the image of God" for His purpose. Instead, we sometimes try to make them in our own image, whether it is the image of who we are, or who we wish we were. Frustration often comes as the result of our lack of understanding of the development of our child's own personality.

The most frequently quoted verse in all of Scripture for parents is Proverbs 22:6—"Train up a child in the way he should go, and when he is old he will not depart from it." Hebrew scholar Franz Delitzsch, explains this verse as follows:

> The education of youth ought to be conformed to the nature of youth; the matter of instruction, the manner of instruction, ought to regulate itself according to the degree of development which the mental and bodily life of the youth has arrived at.[1]

Many psychologists have said that 85 percent of a child's personality is formed by age six. Those years of six and under, however, are the most compliant years. How can the remaining 15 percent cause so much trouble? Very often it is the result of a parent who cannot accept that 85 percent for what it is. The person *you* think the child should be can be very different from the person *the child* thinks he should be, and even from the person he really *is*.

What Christ Is Doing

In my ministry's office, I have a policy of hiring young men who are studying for the ministry. More often than not these young men have made a profession of faith in one of our crusades. Frequently they have a background of drug or alcohol abuse. These fellows are frequently "rough around the edges," so to speak. Dress and hair style are often the last to change, even though a young man's heart is on fire for the Lord.

I have yet to tell one of these young men, "Cut your hair. Clean up your appearance and how you dress." Instead, we have focused on what Christ is doing in their lives and what it means to be totally obedient and yielded. One by one these young men have cut their long hair, and it has always been on their own initiative. They say simply that the Lord impressed them to do it.

Of course, it may be easier for me to wait than it is for some dads. After all, I, too, was one of those kids with long hair waiting for God to do a work in my heart. Growing up as a young boy, I used to throw rocks at the buses of the Baptist church when they came through my neighborhood. Twenty years later, I was the pastor of that church!

I became a Christian at age seventeen. With long, scraggly hair and needle marks up and down my arm, I began to attend Bible studies. Various people came along who literally pointed me in the right direction. One of those was Dr. H. Fred Williams, a professor who taught a Bible class I attended. Fred never told me to cut my hair or change my clothes, but he loved me into doing both. Every Monday night after class he would come to my home and sit with my wife and me. He taught me God's Word on issues such as tithing, and he later gave me my first chance to preach.

The day came when I put on a tie, cut my hair, and became pastor of the Friendship Baptist Church, a small rural congregation. Instead of pushing me into conformity, Fred enticed me into growing into obedience and faith. He told me in later years that he was so intrigued by my desire to learn that he felt sure God was going to do the teaching. So you see, *I am living proof that God is never finished with a young life.*

When parents communicate to a young person that the most important trait to them is compliance to their rules rather than learning to make responsible decisions, walls go up between them, resentment sets in, and a battle of wills ensues. Our job is to point out the correct path. Just as a ship must have a port of destination, a navigation plan, and emergency flotation gear, parents must furnish all this in a spiritual sense to their teenager. Each day they are attacked by waves of temptation: drug use, sexual promiscuity, and just plain settling for second best. The If-It-Feels-Good-Do-It mentality permeates their environment. It is our job to provide an accurate compass that will enable each teen to "stay on track."

To Equip for Battle

As parents look toward the warfare that lies ahead, they must not neglect to equip their children with what they need to win. Peter, during a period of great persecution, admonished believers to conduct themselves with courageous faith. Knowing the difference between right and wrong is not enough. He told them, and now he tells us, how we must "add to your faith virtue, to virtue knowledge, to knowledge self-control, to self-control perseverance, to perseverance godliness, to godliness brotherly kindness, and to brotherly kindness love" (2 Pet. 1:5–7).

Faith

In the ladder of spiritual excellence, Peter very carefully selected faith as the first rung. Both you and your child must have a firm footing on this step before climbing any higher.

Before we can enable our children to make the journey of faith, we must be sure that they have been partakers of saving faith. So many grow up coasting downhill on their parents' faith. All is fine until they hit the bottom and find they have no power of their own. It was said of the sons of Eli the priest, "Now the sons of Eli were corrupt; they did not know the Lord" (1 Sam. 2:12). How is it that a godly priest could raise ungodly sons? Simply stated, they had no personal relationship with the Lord.

This same scenario is present in the twentieth century. It is an astounding fact that after leaving home, an overwhelming majority of students cease to attend church. It is essential for our children to develop a personal walk and relationship with the Lord. Leaving home should never mean leaving God.

Virtue

Virtue is moral excellence. God has set a goal for every child, and that goal is moral freedom. This goal determines what decisions are made in the critical areas of life, such as in the matter of sex before marriage. I have heard pastors and other church leaders talk about sexual purity in such drab tones they gave the impression that kids basically have to put their lives on "hold" until they finally cross the marriage threshold.

We need to let young folks know that there is something exciting about obeying God. Teach them to use all that energy in a positive and wholesome fashion. Obeying the Lord in tempting situations is a badge of courage, attained through striving for moral excellence. It is not a burden, it is freedom, because once the decision has been made, the pressure becomes easier.

Knowledge

In Peter's list of battle equipment, knowledge refers to spiritual understanding, the ability to live skillfully in difficult days. Bill Gothard offers this:

God's Will—Exactly what I would choose if I knew all the facts.

God's Way—Exactly the opposite of my natural incli-
nations.

God's Work—Exactly what Jesus would do if He were
in my situation.[2]

Knowledge of the Word of God concerning the daily issues
of life is preparation. Many a struggle, many a decision need never
even be considered when we know the Word of God and the Will
of God for every believer, which has been clearly given to us.

Temperance

This is self-control. We must help our children realize that
their appetites and ambitions are God-given, and therefore must
be under His control. The great theologian of yesteryear, William
Barclay, calls temperance "the ability to take a grip of oneself."[3]
Our responses determine the results.

Think with me for a moment about the circus elephant.
Weighing in at more than two thousand pounds, it stands compli-
antly, tethered only by a small chain. The elephant has the power
to break the chain and pull up the stake, but its power is under
control.

Perseverance

While *patience* may be too passive a definition of the word
perseverance, the meaning is essentially the same. Ours is an instant society—microwaves "nuke" our meals in minutes; fax machines transmit messages across the country and the world in less
than a minute; we are one-minute managers, ever searching to
find ways of getting the job done faster and easier.

We are accustomed to seeing life's major problems worked
out in a thirty-minute sitcom. Anything beyond that in normal
life seems impossible to deal with. Union strikes, often based on
the attitude that "If we don't get our way, we quit," are so common they are often ignored by the press.

With this backdrop for everyday life, we can understand the
significance of the fact that the Greek word for patience literally

means "abiding under." Patience is the ability to stay under the load and to continue onward and upward. It means not quitting when the going gets tough.

It is imperative to both demonstrate and teach our children perseverance. They need to see us bearing up under the pressure of day-to-day conflicts in finances, career, and marriage. Christian steadfastness finishes the race.

Godliness

Godliness refers to character that displays the presence of God. While we concentrate fully on telling our children how to be good, we may never explain Who the standard of measurement is.

Someone has said that godliness is "the divine response to how others treat us." I would add, especially to those who wrong us or mistreat us.

One day my daughter came home from school in tears. "I wasn't talking, but the teacher said I was and now I've got detention! I can't stand her!" Being the protective father that I am, I wanted to drive over to that school, grab that teacher up and exclaim, "How dare you punish my daughter for something she didn't do!" But I didn't, for two reasons.

First, I know my daughter well enough to know that if she wasn't talking *this* time she probably was another time when she didn't get caught. I explained this to her and we both had a good laugh about the truth of that statement.

Second, the Bible reminds us over and over to seek the example of Christ, "who, when He was reviled, did not revile in return" (1 Pet. 2:23). Beyond that we are told, "For what credit is it if, when you are beaten for your faults, you take it patiently? But when you do good and suffer, if you take it patiently, this is commendable before God" (v. 20).

The Scripture is really the only source of wisdom and authority I believe I can honestly recommend to my daughter. In this light, that detention now became an opportunity to be Christ-like, and that gave it purpose.

William Barclay describes the great characteristic of godliness as a two-way street: "The man who is godly always correctly

worships God and gives Him His due; but he always correctly
serves his fellow men and gives them their due."[4]

Brotherly Kindness

This trait refers to sacrificial sensitivity to those in your path.
The word translated "brotherly kindness" is *philadelphia*, from
which comes the name of our city of brotherly love. Part of what
it means to raise a "good" child is to raise him or her to be sensitive to the feelings and the needs of others. I honestly believe that
this is more caught than taught.

When we think of brotherly kindness today, we think of
feeding the homeless or lending a hand to those in need. Certainly we cannot claim to be a follower of Christ if we do not attempt to do these things.

In our home, we have learned that a Sunday school lesson
is not enough. To act upon what we teach, we have made it an
annual tradition to work as a family in our church's "Feast of
Plenty." Each Thanksgiving our church offers thousands of less
fortunate men, women, and children a home-cooked, hot, tur-
key dinner with all the trimmings. Blankets and clothing are
given out as well. Each of us chooses a job—one helps serve
food, one works with smaller children, one sorts clothing, and
all of us pray. It is brotherly kindness in action, and the kids feel
good about giving of themselves. They also come away with a
spirit of thanksgiving for what they have. It puts gratitude in
their attitude.

We pray as a family daily that we might be used in some
small way to make a difference in a life. It may be sharing a bit of
food, giving a lonely child a hug, handing down some clothing or
toys, or offering an uplifting word of encouragement. The idea is
to be aware of the needs of others and to be willing to meet them.

Love

This essential attribute means doing what's right regardless
of the cost. Love is sacrificing to meet the needs of others. As is

often said, love is not a feeling, it's an act of your will. It's a verb, not a noun. It's the public testimony to others of who God is.

Even though 1 Corinthians 13 portrays love in a poetic and beautiful way, it has become more reading material than living material. The Phillips translation of this passage demonstrates the act of giving love and the feeling that results:

> Love is slow to lose patience. Love looks for ways to be constructive. Love is not possessive. It is neither anxious to impress nor does it cherish inflated ideas of its own importance. Love has good manners. Love does not pursue selfish advantage. It is not touchy. It does not keep an account of evil or gloat over the wickedness of other people. Love is happy when truth prevails. Love knows no limit to its endurance. There is no end to its trust. There is no fading of its hope; it can outlast anything. It is in fact the one thing that still stands when all else is fallen.[5]

To Make Complete

Luke 2:52 makes the interesting observation that the adolescent Jesus "increased in wisdom and stature, and in favor with God and men." This is the complete cycle of adolescence. We want to prepare youth for adulthood *mentally* ("in wisdom") *physically* ("in stature"), *spiritually* ("in favor with God"), and *socially* ("in favor with men").

Increasing in Wisdom

Wisdom is not limited to learning facts, but it does contain knowledge. Webster's defines wisdom as "the power of true and right discernment; good practical judgment; a high degree of knowledge." A more common definition is increasing in knowledge and in the ability to use that knowledge morally and successfully. Wisdom is the catapult to excellence in living.

Before we can enable our teens to be wise, we must help them to expand their knowledge. Teach them how to study, how to take notes, and how to make learning enjoyable. If we motivate teens properly instead of just pressuring them, our teens will expand their learning.

The importance of reading cannot be overemphasized. Our youth will become tomorrow what they read today. Our example is paramount in making reading an enjoyable pastime. We can encourage them to read by reading ourselves.

We can also offer variety in what they read. If you have a child who doesn't like to read, let him read what he likes. While I wish my children would read more of the classics and more biographies, I am pleased that they enjoy reading almost anything. There is no harm in throwing in light reading, such as sports and teen magazines, or teen novels (provided their content is acceptable). Remember, the goal is to get them to enjoy reading, not necessarily to prescribe to a literary diet of our choosing.

The brain expands its usefulness as it is fed new information. The rate at which it expands varies, for every child is on his or her own timetable. I often use myself as an example. In high school, I was a D and F student. I graduated from high school in 1971 (I think they only let me graduate to get rid of me). But four years later I graduated from Charleston Southern University *cum laude*. I hated history as a teen, but I minored in it in college. Today I am a voracious reader. I have learned from experience that a slower learner can accomplish as much or even more than the quicker student. It just may take a little more time!

Increasing in Stature

It may seem that we need do nothing to encourage kids to grow physically. They outgrow shoes and clothes faster than we can replace them. But it is our job to help them to do so gracefully.

Surprisingly, many adolescents are unaware of the increased need for hygiene during adolescence, of the changes taking place in the body, and of the benefits of exercise. It may seem redundant to say to a fifteen-year-old, "Wash your face, brush your teeth, and take a bath every day," but it may be necessary.

It is never too early to teach nutrition and how to stay on a balanced diet. Gaining excess weight in adolescence can cause health problems during the adult years. Nagging will not help, but example, education, and motivation will. My goal was to be more of nudge than a nag. Exercising as a family is fun and beneficial, not only physically but in bonding together and making memories.

Be creative. Weeding the garden may be fun one week, but not every week. Hiking through the neighborhood, basketball at the park, bowling, skating—all of these provide good exercise, and they're fun.

One summer our daughter went to a sports camp where she learned to play a variety of games, was introduced to exercise equipment, and was instructed in nutrition. She loved learning about the sports without the pressure of being on a team immediately.

Dr. Kenneth Cooper, known as the father of the aerobics movement and the founder of the world-renowned Cooper Clinic in Dallas, Texas, believes exercise acts as an antidote for emotional disturbances and can improve intellectual capacity. Because of its positive benefits, exercise is essential in the life of a growing teen.[6]

In Favor with God

This is usually the last area in which the teen begins to show independence, but it is the polestar around which all the rest of life will revolve. This is the glue that holds a life together. Yet I am constantly amazed that many parents who are diligent in other important areas are neglectful in this integral area.

I stress its importance because of the teaching of the Scriptures and the testimony of experience. We humans were created with a God-shaped vacuum inside. As Augustine said many centuries ago, "Our hearts are restless until they find their rest in Him." How then can we fail to see that this need is met in the lives of our own children?

Helping your child develop spiritually is also the greatest way to help her grow up emotionally sound, too. A healthy love for the Lord results in a healthy self-image and in healthy respect for others.

A personal relationship with the living Lord must be taught by example and actions. The importance of prayer, obedience to the will of God, and repentance of sin are necessary elements of the spiritual life. Through your example in these areas, your children will develop a relationship with God of their own.

Memorizing Scripture may be the most effective tool for spiritual growth we can provide our children. As Paul reminded Timothy, "from childhood you have known the Holy Scriptures, which are able to make you wise" (2 Tim. 3:15). We can find no greater source of strength in making correct decisions and overcoming temptation than through Scripture memorization.

Memorized Scriptures can also provide a vital resource for future challenges. Kathy Koob, one of the Americans held hostage in Iran for more than a year (1979–80), remembers, "I filled my days by searching my mind for Scripture verses and hymns I had learned as a child."[7]

As our children commit passages to memory, and as we pray for them, the Word of God is illumined in their hearts and minds. "For the word of God is living and powerful, and sharper than any two-edged sword, piercing even to the division of soul and spirit, and of joints and marrow, and is a discerner of the thoughts and intents of the heart" (Heb. 4:12).

In Favor with Man

It may seem redundant to speak of teaching a teen to talk, but many have never learned how to participate in a conversation. The basic manners and courtesies must be practiced. A light role-playing time prepares the adolescent to be prepared for various types of conversations and relationships, from the tough-talking bully to the class gossip to a church social.

Preparation is absolutely essential when it comes to the "boy-girl thing." You wouldn't send your child into the cold without a coat, to school without breakfast, or try to fight an illness without medication. Why would you send her into the world of dating without a thorough understanding of what dating is? Your son's football team would never dream of playing a game without practice. Would you send him unprepared into the drama of dating—a game that plays for keeps?

We have used the word *preparation* over and over for parents, but now we must endear the word to our children. Dating is *preparation for marriage*. Who they date today could affect the rest of their lives. One easy guideline is to never date anyone you wouldn't marry. Never bite the apple until you've checked for worms. The Scriptures teach that the purpose of dating is to get to know each other emotionally and spiritually. Marriage is the time to get to know each other physically as you spend the rest of your lives together. One overwhelming reason why there is a divorce every twenty-seven seconds and that one out of two marriages end in divorce can be traced back to dating habits—not getting to know the real person. The physical attraction looms so large in many dating relationships that it becomes the only real issue.

A girl feels that having a boyfriend means she is loved, and this boosts her value to others. Having a boyfriend is so important to them that more than 75 percent of teens say they would go out with someone even if their parents objected. Now, they think, *the fairy tale can begin to come true*.

Teens sometimes fall into a trap we call "missionary dating." The Christian teen dates the non-Christian with the intention of winning the unbeliever to Christ. Sometimes it works this way, but it is a dangerous game. With the extremely high incidence of date rape and teenage pregnancy, I have to vote against this practice. It is simply not necessary to date in order to accomplish the goal. There are many group activities where the gospel can be presented and Christian influence made.

Adolescence is a time of inevitable change in every way—in appearance, in personality, in spiritual awareness, and in social and family relationships. We cannot be so concerned about *what* teens are *doing* that we don't see *who* they are *becoming*.

Leading a Child to Independence

Paul and Jeannie McKeen have developed the following checklist for parents as a guide:[8]

Spiritual Development

☐ Knows how to study the Bible

☐ Has a "quiet time" with the Lord

☐ Has a general working knowledge of Scripture

☐ Is developing as a person of faith

☐ Has a strong concept of who God is

☐ Has a strong understanding of who he or she is in Christ

☐ Is consistently growing in the ministry of the Holy Spirit

☐ Is a person of prayer

Physical Development

☐ Accepts himself physically as a gift from God

☐ Understands and practices personal hygiene

☐ Maintains proper weight for his age

☐ Keeps a regular physical fitness program

☐ Maintains a good diet

☐ Has at least one sport to develop in

☐ Has regular medical check ups

☐ Maintains a good appearance

☐ Has a biblical perspective of sex

Intellectual Development

☐ Has working knowledge of basic academic skills

☐ Has read world classics

☐ Has general grasp of world history and current events

☐ Knows how to find needed information

☐ Knows how machines work

☐ Knows how to drive

☐ Has a practical knowledge of general skills

☐ Is developing creatively

Social Development

☐ Understands the biblical motivation for relationships

☐ Takes responsibility, as part of society, for actions

☐ Is confident in the role of host/hostess/guest

☐ Knows common etiquette and courtesies

☐ Is confident in making introductions

☐ Is able to relate to various age groups

☐ Puts others at ease because he/she is at ease.

5

How Do You Spell *Problems?*

Eight Issues Kids Struggle with Most

The results of a survey that I have given to thousands of teens across the country boil down to eight issues they wrestle with most. These are not isolated issues, but rather universal ones facing our most precious commodity—our children. Don't be naive and think, My child would never . . . Satan goes after every child. We cannot leave any of them to fend for themselves.

The eight issues can be summarized with the acronym PROBLEMS:

Peer pressure

Relationships

Overall attitude

Boredom

Learning

Esteem

Mind-altering drugs

Sex

Peer Pressure

How many parents have wailed, "He's really a good kid. He just got caught up with the wrong crowd!"

Psychologist Clyde Narramore convincingly argues that teens desire peer approval more than parent or adult approval. They are preoccupied with being accepted by the gang, particularly since this is the age when family relationships may be strained the most.

Now more than ever it is urgent that you know your child's friends, not by prying and investigating, but by an "open-door" policy in your home. The home should be the place where friends enjoy coming.

The shyest boy in the class may suddenly choose to hang out with the wildest one in order to live out a sense of adventure vicariously. The stress of keeping up her grades may cause an excellent student to find friendship with someone who barely gets by academically in order to take the pressure off. If children feel like "losers," they will probably try to find another "loser" with whom they can hang out. When you sense that your child is choosing the wrong kind of friends, try to find out why.

In his book, *Parenting by Heart*, Ron Taffel says that a family needs to act as a sort of "empathic envelope." This envelope is made up of the values, hopes, and aspirations of the parents. Ideally, it will contain and support the children until they go on to make families of their own. When our children reach adolescence, however, they often wish to slip the bonds of our envelope. This is especially true in dysfunctional families. In these situations where the envelope has been ruptured, children will seek to have those needs met by their peers. Taffel goes on to say that a peer group is basically an empathic envelope without adults.[1]

Everyone wants to belong, and some teens will do anything to fit in. I remember one girl whose parents would not let her grow up. They made her dress like a little girl; she was not allowed makeup of any kind, and she was forced to come home immediately from school every day. They were trying to protect her by keeping her in a box. This young lady felt so very out of place (and she was) in her school that she began doing just the opposite. As soon as she was dropped off at the bus stop, off came the little-girl clothes. Buttons were unbuttoned a little more and skirts were yanked higher. Then out came the makeup, lots of it! She ended up hanging out with the most promiscuous girl in the school and running off with her at every opportunity.

I wonder if as Christians we concentrate too much on "looking" like Christians on the outside instead of "acting" like Christians from within. Studies indicate that the urge or drive for affiliation is especially intense when an individual is undergoing an anxiety-producing experience caused by problems at home, or by physiological changes. The constant carousel of change keeps many teens from ever standing alone on the solid rock of Christ.

Relationships

During these years, your teen will crave friendships. All around him friends will be laughing together, making plans together, and sharing the most embarrassing and intimate incidents. Having good friends is significant in the formation of a teen's self-concept.

Although I pray and counsel with many teens, one young man in particular touched my heart. He came to me wearing a T-shirt that declared "Satan Rules." He shared with me a sad but all too familiar story.

Because of a job transfer, the family moved during the middle of his junior year of high school. For various reasons, this young man had a difficult time adjusting to his new environment. As is often the case, the only peers who showed an interest in him were those involved in drugs, drinking, and heavy metal music. Listening to the lyrics of rebellion and suicide over and over for hours in solitude, he soon became fascinated with the occult.

Standing before me, this young man desperately wanted to turn his life around by giving it to Christ. His only stumbling blocks were his relationships. He knew this decision would alienate him from his current friends, and he feared that the straight Christian kids would not welcome him. For this young man, relationships determined much of the course of his life.

We can begin now to pray for Christian friendships for our children, asking God to place those in their lives who will be a blessing and will be blessed. Pray for all types of friendships—with adults as well as peers. A good friend is a sign of acceptance, of love, of self-worth.

Overall Attitude

Just when I think I'll never be shocked again, I am once more appalled at the hardness of some teens' hearts. Things we used to be ashamed to talk about, let alone do, are now laughed about and even bragged about. Our children will hear more filth at school and see more on television than most adults can ever imagine.

The new awareness of evil and the increase in temptation can lead to depression. If an adult is depressed, we can see a definite change or signal, but since adolescence is a time of constant change anyway, a parent may be the last one to understand or sense the teen's depression.

One counselor told me that some parents were so angry at their son for being depressed that they tried to shame him out of it. "You have everything," they said. "We've given you everything. What in the world do you have to be depressed about?" The guilt they put on this poor child kept him locked in still more depression. How could he make them understand if he himself didn't understand?

Adolescence is a time of constant mood swings brought about by rapid physical change and a delicate self-esteem. One sure sign of depression is an otherwise compliant, easy-to-get-along-with teen who becomes easily irritated or hostile. She has not gone from a good kid to a bad kid, but from a carefree kid to a depressed one. There may or may not be a cause to pinpoint, and it is more than likely temporary. Either way, the depression should be taken seriously by both the parent and the teen.

It is normal for adolescents to experience some degree of depression, but when does it become dangerous? Any one of the following phrases signifies a call for help: "It doesn't really matter what happens to me." "What have I got to lose?" "I'll try anything once." "I don't care anymore." "It's too hard. I give up." "I didn't think anybody would notice."

An American Home Economics Association survey of 510 high school juniors and seniors showed that almost six in ten had a friend who had thought of suicide or had actually committed suicide. Those stakes are simply too high to gamble with. Communication is essential and counseling assistance from a minister, school counselor, or other professional would be helpful.

Boredom

Teenage boredom signifies a lack of goals. This is reflected in their common complaint, "There's nothing to do."

What do teens do when they have nothing to do? Usually they watch television. A U.S. Department of Education study concluded that teenagers between the ages of twelve and seventeen watch television an average of twenty-two hours per week during which advertising takes up about four hours (almost 20 percent) of that time. The study also concluded that the more television teens watched, the lower their writing ability. Seventeen-year-olds who watched six or more hours of television per week scored about 10 percent lower on a writing test than those who watched only two hours per week.[2]

In a day and age of advanced electronic and computer games, multiscreen movie theaters, satellite dishes, and entertainment galore, today's teens are still complaining about nothing to do. Full of energy and stimulated by the newness of all that comes to them daily, they are full of great expectations for life. They have not yet learned that life cannot be one giant roller-coaster.

In addition, so much of their life is in transition, and waiting for the next thing to happen makes the boredom feel like forever. The contemporary question, "What's happening?" may mean more than we think. All of the ads tell teens that life is an exciting party. So in their minds they must be occupied, challenged, and laughing every moment. When realism sets in, it often brings boredom.

This is not to say that complaining of boredom is only a negative. Not at all. It can be a positive signal to find new challenges, engage in responsibility, and set new goals. The parent who complains in return, "When *I* was your age, I didn't have time to be bored," or "How can you be bored with all the stuff you have?" is skirting the issue. That teen will find a challenge somewhere. He will fill his time. It is up to us to be sure that this temporary slowdown does not become the first step on the wrong road with the wrong friends. The key word here is *direction*.

Learning

The educational system has become creative in coming up with new names for children with learning difficulties. They are "slow learners," "special ed" students, and "underachievers." Finally, after many years, educators are recognizing that many "normal" kids have abnormal learning patterns. They simply learn differently. Instead of butchering their self-esteem by giving them cookie-cutter work they cannot do, we need to become sensitive to the individuality of kids, particularly in their learning styles.

Even though my oldest daughter is hearing impaired, she is an auditory learner. That means she learns best by hearing facts explained. My younger daughter and I are both visual learners. If I can't see it in print or visualize it in my mind, I can't grasp it. Still others may be kinesthetic learners—they need hands-on learning that involves working through the motions.

The same is true for study skills. One father said that his son is so easily distracted by noise and movement that he must have some background music so that he can tune out everything else and concentrate on study. For me, memorizing means getting up and acting out the words. Most teens prefer an informal, unstructured atmosphere. Studying with a friend is a teacher-student type of role play that allows time to think and to interact. Allowing older students to tutor younger students works well for both of them. The older student learns self-esteem and serving and is also able to review subjects. The younger student enjoys the peer relationship and can relate easily to the person close to her age. Encourage your child to use her own learning and study styles.

Do not hesitate to have your child tested to pinpoint his learning style. He will be relieved to know that there is a reason schoolwork has been difficult. From there you can proceed to emphasize the positive—what he can do right.

Children retain:

10 percent of what they read

20 percent of what they hear

30 percent of what they see

50 percent of what they see and hear together

70 percent of what they say

90 percent of what they say and do at the same time

In the popular video series "Where There's a Will There's an A," Claude Olney says,

> Recent research reveals several other important IQ's. *Street Smart* thinking is a different skill that's not even considered on standard IQ tests. Nor is *Practical Intelligence,* which is needed by the successful executive. *Creative IQ,* the hallmark of outstanding artists and musicians, is not measured. The *Coordinative IQ* of the skilled surgeon is missing. So is the *Athletic IQ* of someone like a professional golfer, who uses numerous computations in hitting a ball, taking into account variables such as wind and distance to solve a very complex series of mental problems, all in a split second.

If you see your children's grades slipping or notice some peculiar difficulties in certain subjects, don't hesitate to find help. *They should never feel "stupid" or be publicly embarrassed by what they cannot do.* No matter the schedule, learning differences require time for extra assistance. A weekly schedule of homework, quizzes, and projects written down neatly for quick referral will benefit both the parent and child. Often a very small adjustment will make a big difference in learning how to study and take notes, reviewing in smaller segments, understanding what the teacher expects, and so on.

Esteem

Dr. Paul Meier, co-founder of the nationally renowned Minirth-Meier Clinic, believes that all emotional pain ultimately comes from three root sources: (1) lack of self-worth, (2) lack of intimacy with others, and (3) lack of intimacy with God.[3]

It seems impossible that a young man or a young woman living in a family of love, attending a church with an active youth group, surrounded by people daily, could feel lonely and have low self-esteem. Yet it happens all the time, and parents are often the last to notice.

Students face intense scrutiny on a daily basis by both teachers and their peers. The teacher marks only their wrong answers, and they are graded and evaluated only by what they cannot do. Attention is given when a problem is caused or revealed. These are all negative markers that label and threaten the everyday life of teens.

Furthermore, their peers stand by to see what kind of clothes and shoes are worn, who is or isn't talking to each other, whether a hair style is current, and in general determine whether someone is labeled as "cool" or not. A teen who is "in" one day might be ostracized the next. Not a very encouraging way of life, is it?

After school, teens return home to their parents. There, if parents have unrealistic expectations for their children, they end up feeling like failures once again.

Every person must come to the understanding that self-esteem is not based on performance but on God's love and purpose for us. This cannot happen if we allow our approval of the child to rise and fall on every test score or athletic event.

Self-esteem is based in part on realizing our own uniqueness. When my daughters ask why about how different one is from the other, I reply, "That's just the way God planned it." Teens must believe that God never makes mistakes in the plan He has for us and that He wants to use each of us just as we are.

Teens must understand there is nothing we can do to make God love us any more. They must feel the security of knowing there is no accomplishment necessary to gain their parents' love. *Acceptance from immediate loved ones is the beginning of acceptance of self.*

Mind-altering Drugs

Drug abuse—which includes alcohol abuse—shatters our families, our finances, and our future. While illegal drug use is on the decline, alcohol use among teens continues to climb at an alarming rate. Still, the threat and temptation to use drugs are out there. In a Gallup poll released in 1989, more than 4 million children, ages thirteen to seventeen, said they had been offered illegal drugs in the previous thirty days. In the nineties our children will face more of the same.

Bill Cosby's beautiful daughter, Erinn, granted a magazine interview after being released from a hospital where she underwent treatment for alcohol and drug abuse. "People see Bill Cosby as a super dad," she said. "But I'm proof that drug and alcohol tragedies can happen even in the most loving families." Erinn began drinking at the age of fourteen and went on to drug use, all of which she continued to hide from her parents until college. Her famous parents let her know that they loved her but that she would have to seek help on her own. In the end, tough love won out, and Erinn Cosby is beginning a new life.[4]

Sex

While many "good" Christian girls may innocently fall into a trap of "being in love" when they have their first sexual experience, still more are lost to peer pressure and curiosity. We absolutely cannot ignore the discussion of sex, particularly God's plan for sexual purity until marriage.

In a survey by *Seventeen* magazine, 91 percent of girls and 99 percent of boys wrote to say that they enjoyed sex. Of those who'd had sex, the average age of first intercourse was 15.8 years. Among guys, 21 percent—almost one-fourth—approved of sex simply because it's fun. Only 28 percent of girls and 16 percent of guys said they wouldn't have sex until marriage. Among both girls and boys, 23 percent said parents aren't aware of their sexual activity, and 20 percent said they know more about sex than their parents do.

The sexual message is a confusing one. The previously mentioned survey by the American Home Economics Association also reported that one in three teens has a friend who has been sexually abused. Twenty percent of boys and 50 percent of girls say they have been pressured into having sex. Date rape has now become a very real and very frightening possibility.

With the constant sexual innuendo of movies and advertising, the blatant and crude discussions among peers, and the glamorization of sex at every turn, can we really say to our teens, "Don't think about sex. Just be good"? *We must not only teach them to say no, we must do our best to empower them to say no as well, offering both the wisdom of why to say no and the wisdom of how to do it.*

Delicate Topics

Many parents feel especially uncomfortable when addressing difficult aspects of sexuality such as masturbation or homosexuality. Because we find these topics embarrassing or because we are unsure what to tell our kids about them, we may ignore the matter. But these subjects are matters of intense concern to teens. When we ignore them, we leave our kids to figure out these difficult issues for themselves.

In adolescence, new hormonal activity begins producing sexual desires and tensions. Some believe masturbation provides a healthy outlet for these desires. I believe, however, the Bible discourages masturbation, particularly the compulsive use of masturbation.

Masturbation heightens sexual awareness. Many teens are not yet ready for the responsibility this awareness brings. Masturbation may also increase the sexual drive, which is difficult enough for teens to cope with and control. Masturbation is often accompanied by sexual fantasies, while the Bible clearly states that imagining illicit sex is just as sinful as the act itself. Masturbation is also frequently associated with pornography, which warps sexual desire.

Compulsive masturbation can be a sign of insecurity and unhappiness. It usually indicates underlying disturbances such as loneliness. It typically leads to withdrawal, low self-esteem, and problems relating to others.

Teens need to understand that masturbation in itself does not condemn them as sinful. Temptation becomes sin only when the allurement becomes lust. In the case of sexual temptation, lust occurs when one proceeds to relish the idea of using another person for sexual gratification. Improper sexual desire, however, may signify the need for a change of social habits or reading materials. Vigorous physical exertion may be helpful in controlling sexual desires. So can new goals, hobbies, and interests. Healthy friendships and family relationships are essential, as are a guarded mind and spiritual growth.

Another sexual question that needs to be answered for teens is that of homosexuality. Modern teens may be confused on this subject, but they needn't be. The Bible is crystal clear in condemning it. When mentioned in the Bible, homosexual behavior is followed by the judgment of God. Examples of this are found in Genesis 18–19, Leviticus 18, and Romans 1:24–28. There are people who distort the clear message of these passages and claim they do not mean what they say. Do not fall for it. The Word of God speaks clearly and does not require any special "knowledge of the culture" or any special interpretation. All you have to do is read carefully and let the Scripture speak for itself.

If you think your child is struggling with homosexuality, make sure he or she understands the clear biblical message. Without the backing of the Word, condemnation of homosexuality simply becomes our opinion—and parental opinion often loses when it comes up against peer opinion. Remember, however, that the Word of God condemns the sin, not the sinner. Healing and forgiveness are available in Christ. Seek godly counsel for help in this matter.

How Far Is Too Far?

Teens ask me almost daily, "How far is too far on a date?" I give them these guidelines as an answer.

1. *Does the situation I put myself in invite sexual immorality or help me to avoid it?* 1 Corinthians 6:18 says to "flee sexual immorality." We cannot do this if we are tempting ourselves through carelessness.

2. *What kind of reputation does my potential date have?* When you accept a date you are saying in essence, "My values are the same as your values." That in itself can put you in a position you may regret later.

3. *Will there be any pressure to use alcohol or drugs?* We have already discussed the effect of drugs on sticking to moral standards. As your vision becomes fuzzy, so do your decisions.

4. *Am I attracting the wrong type of person* by the message I send by my dress, my actions, the friends I hang out with, or the places we choose to go?

5. *Do I find myself attracted to unspiritual or immoral dates?* If so, stop dating immediately and seek counseling.

6. *Am I aware that sin is first committed in the heart?* "But I say to you that whoever looks at a woman to lust for her has already committed adultery with her in his heart" (Matt. 5:28). Don't flirt with fantasy.

7. *Are we going to the right kind of place for a date?* Never agree to a date at home, especially alone. Don't agree to go parking, even though it's "just to talk." Many good intentions have been forgotten because the temptation and opportunity were too great. Sexual feelings are stirred up that cannot righteously be fulfilled.

8. *Am I doing anything to encourage sexual desire?* Petting with anyone you are attracted to will soon lead to an abused mind, body, and personality, because you have allowed yourself to be "used" by others.

Facing Your Problems

These are the P-R-O-B-L-E-M-S teens are concerned about and face on a daily basis. Theirs is a difficult task—to cross the bridge from child to adult.

Perhaps more jokes have been told about adolescence and more books have been written about this stage of life than any other. Bonaro Overstreet made this assessment: "Of all the curable illnesses that afflict mankind, the hardest to cure, and the one most likely to leave its victim a chronic invalid, is adolescence."[5] By understanding what teens perceive as life's most challenging P-R-O-B-L-E-M-S, we can offer them emotional healing.

6

"He's a Rebel"

How to Handle Conflict with Your Kids

Visiting in a home one evening after a service, I found myself looking at the various family photos scattered throughout the den. One photo struck me in particular, for it was of this lovely Christian family: two dedicated parents in love with each other and their children, a beautiful smiling daughter, and a frowning son.

Even in the one dimension of this photo, and without having met the boy, I could see his depression and his pain. When I asked about him, the mother's countenance dropped immediately, and I thought she would burst into tears. "That's our son, but we don't know where he is." She proceeded to tell me the story of a fun-loving young boy who grew into a sullen, uncooperative teenager. "We don't know where we went wrong."

Taking one glance at the picture, I could see the answer to the mystery of this child. At some point in his young life, something happened that he could not deal with emotionally, but he never told anyone. You could see it written all over his face— "I've quit trying." Sadly, his parents did not see it until it was too late. Or even worse, they saw it but didn't know what to do, so they could only hope it would go away.

I am the first to admit that I have had to read more and work harder at being a good father and a good husband than I read and worked in all my years in college and graduate school. It is imperative that parents understand something about the special nature and problems of the teen years.

Understanding Teens

Teenagers are those exciting and sometimes unusual young people between the ages of twelve and twenty. In the most crucial years of their lives they possess the potential to change the world in which we live . . . or to virtually destroy it. They will make nearly every important decision affecting their entire future during the short eight years of adolescence.

Conflicts between parents and teenagers are not uncommon during these difficult years as the teenager grows from childhood dependence toward young adult independence. A teenager is ascending in independence, and parents are becoming increasingly dependent upon their children. When these two lines intersect (usually about the time the teenager is fourteen), problems often result.

In his role as a counselor, Dr. Ed Hindson relates this common scenario: All too often, an irate parent will bring a teenager into his office, throw him down in a chair, and in essence say, "For eighteen years I have not been able to control this self-centered teenager. Now please do something with him in the next thirty minutes!" Problems that take years to develop are not corrected in a matter of moments. (Of course this does not mean that there is no immediate help available in case of a genuine crisis.)

In the Bible, God refers to all believers as being a "chosen generation" (1 Pet. 2:9). It is clear in this passage that God deals with all born-again Christians as part of the same generation. Therefore, there is no "generation gap" as far as God is concerned. Christian teenagers and Christian parents have every potential to resolve the conflicts that exist between them, because the Spirit of God lives in both of them.

The Chain Reaction of Rebellion

Conflict between teenagers and their parents begins when parents fail to live up to the standard they have established for the family. For example, you want your child to keep her word and be the best she can be without making excuses by comparing herself to others. So when you as a parent break promises or make negative comparisons you may often hurt a child deeply. The result is bitterness and hurt feelings that become the first sparks in a chain reaction leading to a crisis of rebellion.

The Starting Point Is Hurt

Years of ministry have convinced me that the majority of teenage rebellions begin with hurt feelings over something the parents have said or done. It is not the teenager's fault he is hurt, but he must assume the blame if he harbors that hurt and allows it to turn into bitterness, destroying his own spiritual life in the process.

Some teenagers can tell you the exact time, day, and place of the incident with their parents. With detail they can describe the deep pain that eventually led them to reject their own families. Others cannot isolate a specific incident, but they remember a long series of incidents. Either way, the problem produces the same symptoms and results. Hurt harbored in the heart soon becomes bitterness.

Breakdown in Communication

The next link in the chain of rebellion is often *a breakdown in communication*. This can be the first indication something has gone wrong between the parent and child. However, many parents overlook this symptom as if it were merely a "stage" through which the teenager is passing.

Communication often breaks down because the teenager no longer feels confident about "opening up" to his parents. He fears being hurt again; therefore, he keeps his feelings and frustrations to himself. In time this turns into a loss of love and respect.

The loss of respect leads to the next indication of something wrong in the parent-teen relationship—the lack of gratitude. Teenagers are greedy enough to accept the gifts that their parents give them, but not always with the best attitude. The ungrateful spirit may be produced by the inner feeling that the parents are trying to buy back the teenager's love. This only deepens the conflict between parent and teenager as it leads to the parent's playing the old when-I-was-a-kid theme and the child's feeling guilty.

Mom and dad often go into a lengthy dissertation on all the things they had to do without when they were teenagers—how they never had bicycles, cars, baseball gloves, new dresses, stereos, televisions, etc. However, parents should remember that they bought all the material items they are now criticizing their children for having.

Also, your child cannot effectively relate to your childhood because he did not live during that period of time. If you were born during the 1940s or 1950s and your child was not born until the late 1970s, he cannot appreciate your generation just as you cannot appreciate or comprehend the 1920s!

Rejection of Authority

When a teenager loses love and respect for his parents, he will almost automatically begin to reject their authority. This will show up in the symptom of *stubbornness*. The teenager will become increasingly resistant to his parents' demands and regulations upon his life. He may not yet be brave enough to rebel openly, but that is soon to follow.

At this point, the parent has already been given three major flashing "danger signals" that disaster is on the way: communication breakdown, ungratefulness, and stubbornness. Each of these reactions is an indication of a deeper problem within the teenager's life. Taken together, they should be considered a "code blue" alert.

While the parent fears that rejection may be coming, it has in reality already occurred in the teenager's mind! His rejection of his parents' authority soon leads to a rejection of all other adult authority as well. The teenager now finds himself at odds with his pastor, youth director, and teachers.

Having rejected the authority of his parents, the teen needs a new authority factor in his life. At this point, most teenagers establish themselves as that authority. They decide that "me, myself, and I are going to run my own life. No one is going to tell me what to do. I'm going to do my own thing." The establishment of self-authority now sets the teenager at odds with his parents' established authority. This almost immediately results in open rebellion. The teenager is now out of control and will not do what his parents demand of him.

It is at this point that most parents panic and run to their pastor, school administrator, or the police for help. Not realizing that the rebellion has been brewing under the surface for some time (perhaps even years), they usually imply that something drastic has recently gone wrong with their teenager, and they expect other adult authorities to agree.

Having reached the end of their rope, these parents have their greatest difficulty taking any personal responsibility for the condition in which they find their child. Most counselors know that they will never be able to solve a problem between a teenager and his parents until the parents are willing to acknowledge that they are a part of the problem. Only then can they become part of the solution as well.

Rebellion is serious in God's sight. "For rebellion is as the sin of witchcraft" (1 Sam. 15:23). Nowhere does the Bible condone teenage rebellion; in fact, it speaks strongly against it. "He'll grow out of it" may be some of the most dangerous words ever spoken. *Growing out of it is not in question; it is which way he will grow that is the enigma.*

While the teenager must accept personal responsibility for his sinful rebellion, parents must also face their responsibility. Perhaps they have "provoked their children to wrath," or neglected them, or been overly dominant. Without the proper balance of scriptural instruction and effective discipline, the teenager will overreact against his parents. Too often the parent attempts to handle the teenager's stubbornness with arguing and with increased rules and demands, which only increase the rebellious attitude. These measures do not necessarily amount to corrective discipline and often only further alienate the teenager from his parents.

Following the Crowd

Since the teenager is now operating on self-authority, he tends to feel lonely making his own decisions and will automatically look for a psychological support group to justify and reinforce his rebellion. This usually shows up in the form of "having the wrong friends." The wrong crowd always influences him to do the wrong thing, although he may also influence them in the same direction. That is because we choose as our closest friends the people that are most like us. Whether you like it or not, your friends tell a story on you; they reveal what you are really like.

Because of the regulations of the family or a Christian school, your teenager may still conform outwardly to certain demands, but the attitude and appearance of his friends reveal the inner attitude of his heart. The clenched-fist crowd will cause the teenager to clench his fist because he needs to feel accepted by the group.

Facing the Fact of Sin

Understanding broken relationships between parents and teens includes, for the Christian, an awareness of sin. Psychologists use many words for abnormal and unacceptable behavior. But the forgotten word in many circles is *sin*. This biblical expression means "to miss the mark," "to fall short" of the standard of a holy God.

Parents must not feel uncomfortable with this term, because it is the heart of the problem. When kids begin to defend smoking, drinking, and drugs, it is obvious that they are already involved in these things or wish to be involved. Their questions are not really those of genuine intellectual interest, but those of personal defense. People tend to defend their sin, and in doing so reveal what their sin problems really are! A telltale sign is when they protest too vigorously.

The problem with sin is that it only offers pleasure "for a season," and soon leads to guilt and depression. The more a person sins, the more guilt he will experience, and in time he will begin to condemn others.

There are several things you should know about sin. First, realize that there is *pleasure* in sin. Sin is easy, and it is often an attempt to escape from reality by such means as drugs, drinking, and illicit sex. Satan has made these very enjoyable—but only for a time.

Second, note the *pitfalls* of sin. In 2 Timothy 2:26, Paul prays that certain people will escape the snare of the devil, having been taken captive by him to do his will. When you least expect it the devil will pull the rug from beneath you.

Third, understand the *progression* of sin. James 1:14–15 describes this progression: "But each one is tempted when he is drawn away by his own desires and enticed. Then, when desire has conceived, it gives birth to sin; and sin, when it is full-grown, brings forth death." Every kick has a kickback. Sin fascinates, then assassinates . . . thrills then kills . . . enjoys then destroys. Sin will take you farther than you want to go, keep you longer than you want to stay, and cost you more than you want to pay.

Fourth, realize the *penalty* of sin. "The wages of sin is death" (Rom. 6:23). Sin is no respecter of persons. You can come from a good family and be active in church. But "Do not be deceived, God is not mocked; for whatever a man sows, that he will also reap. For he who sows to his flesh will of the flesh reap corruption, but he who sows to the Spirit will of the Spirit reap everlasting life" (Gal. 6:7–8). Your sin will find you out—in your face, in your conscience, some day in your children, and then in judgment.

But God has an alternative. Read the rest of Romans 6:23: "but the gift of God is eternal life in Christ Jesus our Lord." This brings us to the fifth thing we need to understand: There is *pardon* for sin. But pardon can happen in only one way. Jesus Christ came to this earth two thousand years ago, lived a perfect life, and laid down His life in your place. Remember, "without shedding of blood there is no remission" (Heb. 9:22). Christ's death is the payment for all sin—past, present, and future. Each of us—parents and kids alike—must come to a personal understanding of this gift and then individually receive Christ into our hearts. Only then will our family relationships begin to shape up as God intended them.

What Can a Parent Do?

What can you do as a parent if your child is already rebelling against you? While you are waiting for him to change, there are some steps you can take for yourself to facilitate the healing:

1. Admit your failures. Seek your teenager's forgiveness for whatever you have done to hurt him so deeply as to cause his rebellious attitude. Some kids will be able to tell you exactly what you did, while others will not be sure. That hurt must be cleared up before a solution can be reached.

2. Correct the original cause of hurt. Reassure your teenager by your consistent life that you have really changed for the better. Some young people will forgive you immediately; others will tend to wait and see if you are really sincere. They may have felt abandoned, either physically or emotionally, or through broken promises. They may have been so deeply hurt that they are afraid to trust anyone. You must convince your child by your life that you can be trusted and that you do have his best interest at heart.

3. Establish a plan of action. Eliminate all double standards and inconsistencies. Be willing to let your teenager tell you what he really thinks about life. You might as well know the truth and begin facing it now. Talk to him and pray with him regularly. If he or she does not want to pray with you, let your teenager hear you pray for him or her. They need to be aware of your genuine concern. Remember the insight from the medical profession: The longer the problem has lasted, the longer the healing process will take.

4. Be dependable and consistent. Once you begin a new course of action, don't quit. If you give up, so will your teenager. Keep your conscience clear with your teenager at all times, thereby taking away any "excuses" for further rebellion. Remind yourself that Satan, the accuser and enemy of your home, will accuse you on every occasion to your children.

5. Live your convictions at all times. As a parent, you are the key to changing your teenager. He must see God at work in your life until he is convinced that you are for real. What God does in and through you will make all the difference in your teenager's life. Our children need fewer critics and more models.

7

A Matter of Heartitude

What Kids Need Most in a Mom

By Diane Strack[1]

The heart of a woman is . . .
  A candle in the darkness;
    Softness to the harshness of reality;
      Motivation for the weary;
        Soothing to the fretful;
          Encouragement to the downhearted;
            Example to all who look upon her.
She is the heart and attitude of the home; she is "Heartitude."

I can visualize the excitement and drama as Jesus entered the home of Lazarus and his sisters Mary and Martha in Bethany (see Luke 10:38–42). Lazarus, the disciples, and the other guests could scarcely contain their joy, for they had watched as Jesus healed the sick and listened as He stumped the Pharisees. Some of them had themselves performed miracles in the name of the Lord. I can imagine the excited conversation:

    "I was right there. I saw the whole thing!"
    "He spoke directly to me. I've been with Him the longest."
    "Can you believe He is here in our village?"

Singleness of Purpose

Martha is running to and fro, ordering servants about, preparing food, making sure that only the best is served for the

Master. She is certainly doing a good work. She is distracted, the Scripture says, by much business and doing. She takes the position of *talking*. "Jesus, tell her to help me."

In contrast, with singleness of purpose, Mary sits at Jesus' feet to catch every word from His lips. She takes the position of *listening*.

Two women, sisters in fact, in the same house, at the same time, with the same guest, saw two different needs. Martha looked into those tired eyes and thought, "He needs nourishing food, clean clothes, adequate rest."

Mary looked even closer into His soul and thought, "He needs someone to believe in Him, someone to listen." So she sat, doing the greatest work to be done that day, ministering to the heart of the living Lord Jesus.

The New King James Version says that Mary "also" sat at Jesus' feet, hearing His words—implying that Martha had done the same at first. But in the next verse she was distracted by what she believed was more important.

When I began writing this study, I found myself very busy doing some very good things. Teaching and serving at my church, raising my children, and being the wife God called me to be kept me "distracted with much serving." The problem was not that I had responsibilities to attend to; it was the constant thought of them and the way they dominated and drove my life.

I began to feel convinced in my heart that it was time to re-sign much of what I was doing so that I could focus my purpose as a woman more clearly. I was doing a *good* job at most things, but not a *great* job of anything. I seemed to be feeding my children's emotions the same way I was feeding their bodies—with fast food!

For me, it was a giant step of faith to pull back in this way. "What if I stay home and the phone doesn't ring? What if no one calls and needs me to do anything? How will I feel?"

Over and over the words of Jesus rang in my mind: "One thing is needed . . ." He was speaking of a woman with a pur-pose, and I wanted to be that woman. So I set about the business of finding and tending to my personal chosen purpose.

Because I have always believed that setting goals was the way to get things done, I started there. But it wasn't long until I saw that goals must have a source of support. I didn't need goals just then, but a clearly defined purpose. So I began to search for it.

Soon I discovered God's purpose for me: to be a woman of grace and inner peace who shows others the magnificent power of God by my example. Once that became the nucleus of my life, all other points revolved around it and fulfilled that purpose.

Next I filled in the goals that would support that purpose. I considered my home first, then my church, then outside activities. This meant using my best energy for the best tasks. It meant not allowing other people to control my time. It meant extending the goals of excellence and organization into every area of life, no matter how small or how large. It meant appropriating time for a quiet inner spirit, a renewed mind, a healthy body.

In practical terms, all this meant that mom wasn't always tired, in a hurry, on the phone, late for a meeting, or reacting harshly to every word any more. I found that my relationship to my children was a greater delight than I had ever imagined. Looking them fully in the face, smiling, laughing with their silliness, enjoying the daily memories we could build on together increased my sense of purpose. No longer was I writing one thing and listening to another. No longer was I doing one thing and pretending to watch another. It became crystal clear to me that the one thing my children wanted of their mother was for me to *listen*, to be a friend.

For me the transition created immediate relief. I also found that the quiet of *listening* for God's instruction was exciting in itself. As each new opportunity for service came (and they did!), I prayerfully and carefully selected those that would keep me in the focus that God had for me.

Seizing the Opportunity

Because Mary had this singleness of purpose in front of her, she was able to seize opportunities. Later, when Jesus approached His betrayal and subsequent death, it was Mary who anointed His feet with costly perfume and wiped them with her hair (John 12:1–3). When Judas protested, Jesus commended

Mary for seizing a unique opportunity: "You always have the poor with you, but you do not always have me" (12:8).

How many wonderful Christian women are so busy serving the needs of others that they do not see that their own children are perishing in front of their very eyes! They are so busy helping outside the home that they do not see the need inside the home. Everyone at church loves them, but their own children think of them as hypocrites.

Moms can be so busy with other matters that they miss such opportunities as taking seriously the very real feelings of their children—those like a puppy-love breakup (it is real to the puppy), a rejected friendship, name calling on the playground. These are all "little" hurts, but they add up to an unstable heart if we are too careless and too busy to see them.

The days pass so quickly. "Tomorrow, I'll check with Tommy's teacher. I'll find out later why her attitude is like that."

The greatest opportunity you will ever miss is the one in your own home. It has been proven that peer pressure is a major factor in the moral decisions of our youth. We must work harder than ever to give them a feeling of unconditional love and acceptance at home, of secure friendship, of a fun, abundant life. We must communicate to them "I not only love you, but I *like* you!" Then, and only then, will the acceptance of peers seem less important in their lives.

Setting the Mood

As Mary set her heart and mind toward the Lord she loved so dearly, she was able, without a word, to set a mood for the entire room. No doubt the best dishes and the finest food and drink were set upon the tables. There must have been an air of expectation and excitement. It was probably a noisy room, with everyone wanting to talk at once about having been with Jesus and what they saw.

Here sat Mary at the feet of Jesus. First, she poured out only a few drops of oil, and only a few people noticed. Then, as she continued to pour both the costly oil and her heart, the fragrance filled the room. I can picture a few heads turning to see the sight, then a few more. Soon those from the kitchen and other areas made their way in, and slowly the mood of the room changed from noisy chaos to quiet peace. All eyes were now fixed on the Lord Jesus and on the woman of purpose who sat before Him.

This indeed is our greatest joy as mothers, to point our children to inner peace and satisfaction to the best use of their lives. Our methods, however, differ greatly. Note that Mary did not speak a word. As mothers, we are loudly instructing with many words. We give battle orders instead of healing words; there is a war over authority and who is right.

It takes more work to be a woman of purpose in your own home than it does to run a major corporation. Remember, those employees can be fired; they *have* to work or they don't get paid and they no longer have a job. But you must motivate through attitude, example, and prayer. I have a plaque hanging by my bathroom mirror so that I must see it each morning and evening. It says, "A mother's heart is a child's classroom."

When I think of a woman's heart and influence I think of a row of dominoes. Although each one is balanced to perfection, all you have to do is push the lead one and the whole row falls. A mother is that lead domino. As her mood goes, so goes the mood of the home. If she is frustrated, angry, tired, and impatient, the rest of the family will be also. If she is gentle, kind, patient, and loving, so is the mood of the home. Quite a responsibility you say? Yes, indeed. The fact is, whether we accept the responsibility or not does not change the fact that mom's heartitude changes the home.

Look for the little things—lunchbox notes, cards in the mail, private little getaways for a Coke, sensitivity to hurt feelings and the need to talk. My children love to talk about the days when they were small and about memories of years gone by. They remember some of the smallest details—what each was wearing, who said what, how hard we laughed. It reminds me of how sensitive their memories are and how we need to strive to give them good, warm memories as an emotional bank they can draw on in time of need.

At our house from time to time we have what is called "The Church of Being Together." Because Jay is a minister, we are in "regular" church more than most, dressed for the occasion and shaking many hands and greeting many people. But when we have "The Church of Being Together," we are dressed casually and there are no set rules. No one else but family is allowed to attend. Recently when visiting my parents in Florida, Grandma attended in her bathing suit and Grandpa was still in his pajamas, but we had a grand time and videotaped the whole thing. Later we extended it to "The Day of Being Together," with water balloon fights, relay games, and a lot of laughing.

For the church service we make up a program, with each family member taking a part such as special music, leading the choruses, reading the Scripture, and leading in prayer and Bible study, which the girls sometimes like to do. The part that has been the most memorable to all of us is the prayers that we have written as a group and then read together to the Lord. We have kept these to read again and again, as well as pictures of the day and the written program of the service.

I have noticed during these times and other family prayers together that it seems impossible to stay angry at the one you are praying with or praying for. What a wonderful way to dispel the anger and to encourage intimacy and love!

Setting the mood does not mean that everything is always about God or that words are always perfect. Part of setting the mood is helping an angry or hurt child to feel good, to take an insecurity and turn it into a strength, to take fears and turn them to victories. It is dealing with the real everyday issues of life, not in perfection but in wholeness. These are the moods set by the heartitude of a mother.

Working Women

I believe the Scriptures clearly teach that women are to contribute in some way to the family income (see Prov. 31:13–16). The Bible does not give a wrong or a right way—some have in-home offices, others go to the workplace, some sell products to friends, others work by phone. Many women are geniuses at shaving dollars off the budget by planning and organizing each purchase. Others are great do-it-yourselfers and save enough for vacations and extras this way.

I have met many women who sew so beautifully that they save hundreds of dollars and make additional income too. I admire those who care for others' children so that they can continue to spend time with their own. One friend teaches an exercise class one day a week and also does tutoring. Many successful businesses are run from the den or spare room. One woman I met had a minifactory going in the back room where she was turning out accessories for one of the poshest department stores in the country. The possibilities are endless—but so are the traps.

Are you working because you feel the family needs more money, only to find out that you are spending more? Nicer clothes, newer cars, and other extras may be taking your best energy away from your children. By the time you pay for gas, tires, auto maintenance, work clothing, daycare or babysitters, outside lunches, office gifts, and more, is the amount of money left over really worth the energy you are giving to it? What about part-time work and scrimping somewhere else?

If you have evaluated all this and concluded, "Yes, a full-time job works for our family," then you will need to be more organized and creative in your family time than ever before so you can set the mood instead of the mood's setting you. This is doubly true if you are a single mom. You have no choice but to work, yet you have no relief or help with the home.

Although women set the mood, they also *react* to the mood more quickly than anyone else in the house. It's really not fair to the kids that mom is always tired. Poll after poll shows that kids would rather do without a few things and have a happy mom around than a tired one who makes them feel guilty when they need money because she has to work outside *and* inside the home.

It seems odd to me that in a day and time of such advanced thinking in every other area we are still asking women, "What do you do?" Generation after generation has proven that there is no greater work a woman can do than to raise a healthy family. We have tried in our society to bolster the title of "homemaker," but there is still the stigma of, "Oh, is that all you do?"

Various studies have reported that if the homemaker were paid for each of her tasks, she would earn a salary of $50,000 to $75,000. *While that may seem to be an impressive amount, it pales in comparison to the value of a woman to the heart of God:* "Rather, let [her adornment] be the hidden person of the heart, with the incorruptible beauty of a gentle and quiet spirit, *which is very precious in the sight of God"* (1 Pet. 3:4).

I laugh when the doctor hands me a new-patient form with a tiny block of space for "Occupation." I want to go to the receptionist and ask, "Do you have another sheet of paper?" For while I proudly put down "Homemaker," that certainly doesn't give an accurate description of the varieties of duties my occupation requires. Besides—*what we do* should not determine *who we are*.

Keepers of the Springs

Each spring as the mountain snows thawed in the Swiss Alps, pounds of decaying leaves, twigs, and other rubble flowed into the streams that rose from the crystal mountain springs. It was the humble job of the "keepers of the springs" to clear all the rubble and blockage from the streams.

The streams flowed down the mountains and ultimately fed a beautiful lake. Everyone enjoyed the beauty of the lake. Lovely swans glided along in the pure waters and children splashed along the shore. The lake was crystal clear and clean, a thing of beauty and delight.

Over the years, however, the keepers of the springs were ridiculed for having such menial jobs. In time, the keepers began to seek more education to better themselves. They took other jobs, and the streams were neglected. Only a few wise old men refused to give up the job, but when they died the streams carried the spring's debris downstream, and no one gave any thought to their condition.

As time passed, the lake became polluted and covered with a film of scum. The swans no longer glided across the lake nor did the children splash along its shoreline. Instead, the lake was deserted and ugly. Only when their beautiful lake became an eyesore did the people realize the significance of the keepers of the springs. How important their work had been! It would take many years to undo the damage done by a few seasons of neglect.

Mothers are the "keepers of the springs." They guard the purity of the home and the children. If mothers allow themselves to be intimidated into thinking that their work is unimportant, the home will be polluted to the detriment not only of the family, but of the entire nation.

When Jesus was anointed in the house of Simon the leper, just before His death, He said to the indignant disciples, "What this woman has done will also be told as a memorial to her" (Matt. 26:13). If your memorial were written tomorrow, what do you think it would say? Fill in the blank: Mom was always

_____.

The power of a woman's heart. It can change a room. It can change a family.

8

I'll Climb with You

What Kids Need Most in a Dad

Women and children first! Man the lifeboat!"

In times of imminent danger, passengers could always count on the captain of the ship. He was the one who protected them when they were in harm's way. Even if the ship was sinking, the captain was the last to leave, and, if necessary, was even willing to go down with his ship.

This time-honored tradition, romanticized in books and films, was tarnished in August 1991, when the captain of the Greek cruise liner *Oceanos* abandoned his ship off the coast of South Africa with more than 160 passengers still needing evacuation. Captain Yannis Avranos made a cowardly and convenient escape via a rescue helicopter. Howard Chua, in *Time* magazine, reported that "Avronos abdicated the hero role to another. His rationale: 'I wasn't needed on the ship, I could contribute more on land.'"[1]

Unfortunately, that captain isn't the only one who is jumping ship and abandoning those who looked to him for protection. Now, more than ever before, fathers are abandoning the time-honored role of the heroic captain of his ship, the family. When a father fades from the scene, he is abdicating the hero's role to someone else.

When asked "What is the worst thing that could happen to you?" children in counseling sessions answer overwhelmingly, "If dad were to leave us." One little girl told me, "My worst nightmare has already happened. Daddy left mom and me for a girlfriend." The greatest fear—and the greatest potential for permanent harm—is the abandonment of a child by his or her father.

There are two types of abandonment: physical and emotional. One is more obvious, as when divorce or separation occurs. The other is not as easily detected, as when the father is too distant, too unfeeling, too busy to be involved in the life of his children.

Lessons from a Strong Father

Every father must remember that the home is to be a place of affection, protection, imitation, correction, and instruction. This is marvelously illustrated in the biblical account of an incident in the life of Abraham's son Isaac.

A Model for Crisis

In Genesis 26 we read that there was a famine in the land "besides the first famine that was in the days of Abraham" and that Isaac had been pushed by the Philistines to leave and pitch his tent in the Valley of Gerar. What did he do to survive in that land of crisis? Genesis 26:18 tells us,

> Isaac *dug again* the wells of water which they had dug in the days of Abraham his father, for the Philistines had stopped them up after the death of Abraham. He called them by the names which his father had called them.

This moving story has a striking parallel for us today. The example of Abraham (digging wells) during a time of distress (the earlier famine) not only enabled his family to survive that particular crisis, but it also left a legacy that, years later, would save his son and twin grandsons.

Scholars debate the exact method of instruction. Some believe the first famine took place years before Isaac was born, and that Isaac learned of Abraham's actions through his father's reminiscences. Others believe Isaac was an eyewitness to the way his father handled the crisis. Perhaps the way Abraham handled the challenge of the famine was burned into his mind and heart when he drank the first cup of refreshing, life-giving water from the well. At any rate, Isaac knew how his father had faced the challenges of life, and he learned from his example.

As a father you should never forget that you are closely watched during the storms of life. Your children are asking, "Does my dad really know and trust God, or is it all just Sunday school talk?" It is my conviction that God provides children with parents in order for the children to learn and see demonstrated "If God be for you, who can be against you?"

Rest assured that there will be enough times of distress to provide your children with such examples. A layoff, an illness, or even a family reunion with the stress it can bring, will allow you the opportunity to teach in the most effective way—by example. Children need models more than they need critics. *They take in more with their eyes than they do with their ears.*

Good and Bad Examples

Of course, Isaac learned other lessons from his father as well. Ever since that moment on Mount Moriah when Abraham was prepared to offer Isaac on the altar at God's command (Gen. 22:1–19), Abraham's example of faith made a big impression on his son. Abraham's example of faith paid big dividends when Isaac proved himself faithful.

Unfortunately, Isaac also observed his father's weaknesses and repeated them in his own life. Abraham's fearfulness, which led him to pretend his wife was his sister (Genesis 20) cropped up much later in the life of Isaac, who also tried to pass off his wife as a sister (Gen. 26:7–11).

Many parents today know that eerie pain of seeing their mistakes repeated in their children's lives. If you respond to difficulties by procrastinating, lashing out in anger, drowning your pain with substances, or lying and cheating, you are teaching your kids to respond to life the same way.

Isaac had to deal with the tragedy of the Philistines' having stopped up the wells his father had dug. Dad, you must remember that your family has an enemy even more persistent than the Philistines. Be careful that the well of your relationship with God is not stopped up.

Don't Plug Up the Well

There are several ways to stop up a well. In Abraham's day, any enemy could use dirt, debris, and decaying animal carcasses, or he could use gold, silver, or silk. In the desert, these precious items weren't nearly so valuable as water. Today, a father might carelessly allow the fleshly or dirty things of life to taint the wells of example, but it's also possible to allow the things we consider valuable—the pursuit of wealth, for example—to stop up the wells. I am ashamed to say it, but I often pray the least when things are going smoothly. Don't allow the gold, silver, or silk— the very blessings of God—to stop up your well.

The Awesome Task of Fatherhood

The task Isaac faced was awesome, but he went about it with the awareness of the good examples his father Abraham had set. Among other things, he could recall Abraham's faith in God and his love for his family.

Fatherly Affirmation

If you sense a barrenness in your life or marriage, it is time to get on your knees and re-dig the well of faith and family. You must do all you can to meet the needs your child has for this kind of father.

The apostle Paul summarized the basic needs of children that fathers are commanded to meet. First and foremost they are warned, "do not provoke your children to wrath" (Eph. 6:4). He gave this same warning to the fathers in the ancient city of Colossae: "Fathers, do not provoke your children, lest

they become discouraged" (Col. 3:21). The most basic need of
any child is warmth, to be loved with an unconditional love.

This love that molds and shapes is best described by the
phrase "positive affirmation." The greatest danger in parenting
your child is the danger of discouragement. We must encourage
and build up. As a father you hold in your hand the power to beat
your child down or build him or her up. Dorothy Corkhill Briggs's
book *Your Child's Self-Esteem* contains a paragraph that is worth
the price of the book:

> Your child's judgment of himself influences the kinds of friends
> he chooses, how he gets along with others, the kind of person
> he marries and how productive he will be. It affects his creativ-
> ity, integrity, stability and even whether he will be a leader or
> a follower. His feelings of self-worth form the core of his person-
> ality and determine the use he makes of his aptitudes and abili-
> ties. His attitude toward himself has a direct bearing on how he
> lives all parts of his life. In fact, self-esteem is the mainspring
> that slates every child for success or failure as a human being.[2]

Positive affirmation will not just ooze out of you. It is an attitude that requires total concentration. Untold damage is done to
the psyche of a child when you say things like, "You can't do anything right" . . . "You won't amount to a hill of beans" . . .
"You sure are dumb." Such putdowns are difficult to shake and become self-fulfilling prophecies in their lives. Here's a little rhyme
that expresses the correct principle: *If you nag, their shoulders sag.
But if you praise, their shoulders raise.*

The need for affirmation means that the home must be a
kind of "filling station." Ken Blanchard, author of the best-selling
book *The One-Minute Manager*, teaches that employers ought to
be on the lookout for the good things their employees do and to
praise them as often as possible.[3] What works for the office will
work at home. Catch your child doing good and praise him on the
spot.

The "Suzuki Method" is a world-famous technique of teaching people to play the violin. In this method, one of the first
things that children are taught at ages two, three, and four is how

to take a bow. Instructors who use this method realize that when the child bows, the audience will always applaud. They say, "Applause is the best motivator we have found to make children feel good about performing and about themselves."

However, a study by the National Parent-Teacher Organization revealed that in an average American school, eighteen negatives are employed for every positive. Zig Ziglar, in *Raising Positive Kids in a Negative World*, quotes a Wisconsin study which revealed that when kids enter the first grade, 80 percent feel pretty good about themselves, but by the time they get to the sixth grade, only 10 percent have good self-images.[4]

As parents, and especially as fathers, we need to spend less time in negative evaluations and more time in positive affirmations. Are you always majoring on the negatives? Does your child feel that he never quite measures up or that what he does is never enough? Remember, positive affirmation is not based on how much money you spend on your children but how much time you spend with them.

Love that Corrects

Fatherly love must include constructive correction. The apostle Paul not only warned against provoking children to wrath; he urged us to "bring them up in the nurture and admonition of the Lord" (Eph. 6:4 KJV). What does this word *nurture* literally mean for us today? It means training and, more accurately, discipline. A disciplined parent disciplines his children.

The word *discipline* comes from the same word that we get the word *disciple* from. It means to "make a learner." Our motive in discipline is not punishment, but teaching and instruction.

It has been my observation, after eighteen years of ministry, that parents are in for years of headache and heartache if they don't discipline their children. You can sum up a juvenile delinquent in five words: a child left to himself. As Leonardo da Vinci said, "He who does not punish evil, commands it to be done." The Scripture also teaches the necessity of discipline.

But remember that discipline must never be abusive. We must never tolerate any type of abuse, whether physical, sexual, or verbal. You, as a father, are commanded to be a protector and provider. Jesus said, "Whoever causes one of these little ones who believe in Me to stumble, it would be better for him if a millstone were hung around his neck, and he were thrown into the sea" (Mark 9:42). Discipline correctly, promptly, privately, and positively.

To some, positive discipline may sound like a contradiction in terms. Let me explain. Discipline in love and never in anger. Fathers must speak first and spank second. There must always be a warning before there is a whipping. Sometimes parents lash out in anger over something their child has done. Their kids do not have a clue about the reason for the discipline. Instead, they simply learn that if you make dad mad, he will hit you. I hug and explain before and after any correction.

Love that Admonishes

Children are also to be brought up "in the . . . admonition of the Lord" (Eph. 6:4). The word *admonition* literally means "verbal instruction with a view to correction." In other words, this is not what is "done" to a child, but what is "said" to a child.

Fathers should be careful what they say because they will hear those opinions or words again in the lives of their children. To gain more wisdom, I recommend reading a chapter from the Book of Proverbs every day. The entire book can be read as a collection of admonitions and counsel from a father to his son.

It is not enough to discipline a child when he or she does wrong. Your child depends upon you for direction in order to do right. Dr. James Merritt, author and powerful preacher, puts it just this plainly: "If we teach a child nothing about how to live right, we have no reason to complain if he begins to live wrong." In that situation it is not his fault; it is our neglect.

Dr. Jack Graham, pastor of the renowned Prestonwood Baptist Church in Dallas, told me that the reason his children have done so well as they mature is because he has taught them the importance of choosing the right friends. He has constantly brought outstanding Christian athletes to his home and church to allow his children to rub shoulders with them.

The best place for a child to learn the way of God, the will of God, and the Word of God is in your home. Your home and your church should walk hand-in-hand in the raising of your children.

When the time came for my family to move from Florida to Texas, one of our major considerations for choosing a neighborhood was the church we would attend. Our first priority was to find a strong pulpit. Second, we looked for a strong and active youth program with social activities and alternatives for our children. The purchase of a house was secondary to our finding the right church home. We believe that children need consistent exposure to the eternal truths of God's Word and the church should assist the parent in enabling the child to soar spiritually.

Paul's words to the young man Timothy are a good guide even today:

> But you must continue in the things which you have learned and been assured of, knowing from whom you have learned them, and that from childhood you have known the Holy Scriptures, which are able to make you wise for salvation through faith which is in Christ Jesus.
>
> 2 Timothy 3:14–15

The story is told of the youngest of three children who became critically ill. His father, a construction worker, kept a vigil at his bedside. Here the hard-working Christian dad watched helplessly as his son faded away. One fateful day, he received word from the doctor that the boy had passed the point of no return. Stunned, he stood in the corridor, his mind racing with memories of the times he had spent with his son: the fishing and hunting trips, playing catch, and family vacations.

Finally, the moment arrived for the father to discuss death with his son. As he sat on the bed with tears streaming down his face, the boy, ever perceptive, asked, "Am I going to die, Dad? Am I going to leave you and Mom and my brothers? Why are you crying, Daddy?"

After gaining his composure the father asked, "Are you afraid to die, son?"

"No, Dad," the boy replied. "I'm not really afraid, not if God is like you, Dad, not if he is like you."

Although all of us pray we will never have to face a moment like that, it should be the passion of every father's heart to mirror the character of God to his children.

Seeing Through a Child's Eyes

Fathers also need to learn to view life the way their children do. Something magical happens when a dad attempts to see the world through his children's eyes. Have you ever hunkered down on the floor and spent several minutes, or even hours, looking at things in your home from the *physical* perspective of your son or daughter? Seeing the height of a kitchen counter or the top shelf in the refrigerator the way a two-year-old sees it is an enlightening experience. Just imagine how threatening an angry father must look to that little tyke! We already have an adult perspective on the world, but to bring that down to the level our children can appreciate, we have to be able to see as they see.

Priest to Your Children

What does every child need in a dad? I believe your child deserves for you to be their provider, their protector, yes, but also their priest. It is devastating if the father leaves the spiritual responsibility for the family to the mother. America has a generation of children who need to see dad as the spiritual leader in the home. Do you lead during Bible study and prayer time? I am convinced that the time I spend on my knees with my girls will influence them forever. Your home is the battlefield where the war for your children will be won or lost.

A Sunday school teacher was talking to a group of children in her class. She said, "Why do you children love God?"

She received a variety of answers, and the last little boy to answer said, "I don't know why I love God. I guess it just runs in our family."

'I Choose Dad!'

What do kids need most in a dad? They need someone who can be counted on to hold the rope during life.

A rare and beautiful flower grows in the highlands of Mexico. The plant is so rare that it only grows on the side of a certain mountain. The mountain can be climbed, but the side where the plant grows is so steep that only the most experienced climbers can attempt it.

Some time ago this mountain was visited by a group of botanists who wanted some samples of the flower. Visiting a nearby village, they asked a little boy if he would help them. They offered to pay him if he would let them lower him down to the flower by a rope.

The boy answered, "Yes, on one condition."

"Certainly," they replied. "What do you want?"

"I want to pick the person who will lower me on the rope."

The scientists agreed to this. "Who do you want?" they asked.

"My father!"

Would that all dads would have children who would rather trust their lives to them than to any other person in the world.

While preaching a crusade on the island of Oahu, I took a day off and, with my family, headed for the Sacred Falls. A trail that seemed almost straight up led from the parking lot. The lush greenery and native vegetation, the slick rocks, and "almost" slips kept us laughing, smiling, and holding on to each another. We questioned everyone and anyone who was returning from the falls to ensure that this indeed was worth the trip. "And by the way," we would ask, "is it much farther? Are we halfway?"

Even with the assurance that it was indeed a spectacular experience and a sight to behold, we were growing weary when we came upon a sight I shall never forget. There in front of us was a father carrying his teenage son on his back, slowly but surely making his way up the mountain to the falls. It was very obvious by the boy's appearance that he was afflicted with some sort of inflammatory disease. His joints were red and swollen, and he was very thin and frail.

For once in my life, I found myself speechless. I didn't want to go around them for fear of being rude, yet I didn't want to lurk behind them causing them to feel pressured or embarrassed by their pace. Instead, we simply waited and watched. The daddy and the boy continued their way together.

After awhile, we were able to continue our trek. Suddenly the falls appeared before us in all their glory and splendor. After the long, arduous climb, we were anxious to swim in the shimmering pool, which turned out to be unbelievably icy, but a tremendous treat.

As we all enjoyed the refreshment of the water in what seemed like a "Kodak moment," I watched the dad and boy with interest. Very slowly, very patiently, the dad lifted the boy into the ice cold water. The boy squealed with delight, "Daddy, the burning is gone. It doesn't hurt anymore!" The father stood there, beaming. Obviously, the joy of his son was payment enough for all the exertion required to get him there.

When the boy grew tired, his father helped him dress. Lifting him onto his back again, he began the long, tedious descent along the mountainside. We could not help but watch, feeling pity for the boy and admiration for the father.

Again we overtook the man and his boy as we made our way back down the mountainside. This time I was determined not to be intimidated by the awkwardness of the situation. "Excuse me, sir, but I've been watching you and your son. I know you must be exhausted. Could I help carry your son for a little way while you rest? I'm sure he must be heavy, and the trip is a long one."

It didn't take long for the father to reply, "No, thank you. I appreciate your kind offer, but he really isn't heavy to me at all."

He went on to explain that they had made numerous trips to the waterfall together during their vacation for the sole purpose of giving his son temporary relief from the burning pain in his joints.

"To see him laugh and splash about like other kids makes it worth it all."

I left the Sacred Falls that day a better father. I was grateful for having spent quality time making memories with my girls and for having the opportunity to see firsthand *a textbook definition of a father: a protector, provider, and most of all, a friend who will be there at all times—someone who will make the climb with you.*

A parent is one who carries the child's pain to a place of refreshment.

9

A Taste of Heaven

The Home as God Would Have It

The great American theologian and revivalist Jonathan Edwards once said that God intended the home to be a taste of heaven here on earth. Whether that is true or not depends a lot on what parents do to establish the characteristics of a godly home. But before we look at those characteristics, let's look at a family tragedy that makes God's ideal all the more attractive.

A Negative Example

This sad account of a great leader battling with his own son is a classic Catch-22 story. No matter which one wins, both lose. The son wants the father to die; the father wants the son to live. The son wants it all; the father would gladly give it all away to mend his relationship with the son. When the dust of the battle-field settles, twenty thousand men lie dead. The father in his grief inquires about only one.

The biblical narrative about King David and his son Absalom contains elements of splendor, suspense, and sadness. David provides for his son's every need and desire, yet his own example doomed his son to failure. Although Absalom dies in battle, the biblical account reveals that he is lost to David long before the rattling of the sword.

Born as a prince in the royal line, Absalom began life with everything going his way. He was born into a wonderful family.

David loved God, and God was with him. Victory was on every side. The name of the Lord was held in high esteem. As the boy grew, however, his father's walk with God seemed to grow less fervent. At the same time, David's actions began to change the way his son viewed him.

First, Absalom watched from afar as his father took Bathsheba in adultery, had her husband murdered, and then mourned for the death of their son. Without public repentance, David fathered another son, Solomon, and life went on as though nothing had happened. The first lesson is clear: Absalom learned from his father to "talk the talk" and not worry about the walk.

Beginning to be estranged from his father, Absalom enjoyed a close relationship with his sister, the beautiful Tamar. He was outraged when she was defiled by their half brother, Amnon. But once again, Absalom watched as David did nothing. The second lesson: Tolerate sin and do nothing to right the wrong.

A few years later, Absalom invited David and his brothers to celebrate a sheepshearing out in the country. If David had accepted Absalom's invitation instead of sending Amnon alone, everything might have been fine. But David replied, "Let us not all go now, lest we be a burden to you." Lesson three: Family matters are too much trouble; we don't have time.

At this point the story turned brutal. Amnon went to the shearing, and Absalom had him killed. The murder had a dual purpose—removing a rival for the throne and fulfilling Absalom's passion for vengeance. While David was concerned with his own problems, Absalom's heart grew hard, and he became a cold-blooded killer.

There is no "happily ever after" to this story. It ends with the death of Absalom, followed by haunting, painful memories for David. Its moral is that David had failed to pay attention to God's standards for a godly home. Like many parents, he provided for his son's physical needs, even to the point of sacrifice, but he failed to apply his energy to the qualities that would shape his child in a godly direction.

David's story could be our story. We'll drive the same car for an extra year to pay for braces. Somehow we'll scrape up enough for the latest fashions and hair styles. We'll do without some extras in order to pay for a private school. We certainly wouldn't miss an inoculation—and music lessons are a must.

But can we put any less energy and sacrifice and discipline into the emotional and spiritual development of our cherished children? Can we pay any less attention to establishing the kind of home that God would have us establish?

I believe that the qualities that make or break a godly home can be summed up in three A's: atmosphere, appetites, and actions.

The Atmosphere of Your Home

The atmosphere in a home is its overall "feel" or climate—encouragement or discouragement, chaos or discipline, healthy or unhealthy emotions, peace or contentiousness. That basic family atmosphere can make a huge difference in a child's life.

I am working with a young man who wants to commit his life to Christ. He attends church almost every Sunday. But when it comes right down to the prayer of commitment, he holds back. "All my life," he tells me, "my mom has been so harsh and unforgiving. I've never heard a word of praise from her. I've never seen her happy, particularly because of anything I did or said." As a result of this harsh and critical atmosphere in his home, he is not able to accept the unconditional love of God. He is bound in the guilt of hating his mother for what she did to him, and he has great difficulty in sustaining relationships.

An Atmosphere of Affection

An especially important element of a healthy home atmosphere is *affection*. If an overall climate of warmth and caring prevails in a home, many other obstacles can be overcome.

A team of three psychologists representing Harvard University, Boston University, and Adelphi University interviewed 379 moms with five-year-olds in 1951 and followed up with 94 of the kids thirty-six years later. As a result of this study the researchers came to believe that parents who hug, kiss, and cuddle their young children are helping to ensure closer, happier social ties when their kids grow up.

The study showed that physical affection and warmth to- ward kids strongly predicted closer marriages and friendships, bet- ter mental health, and more success at work. It suggested two likely causes for this link between affection in the home and later social skills.

One of these causes was *modeling*. Children imitate the nur- turing they've seen their parents provide. Warm relations at home predict warm relations as adult.

Of course imitation can have both positive and negative ef- fects. Modeling may never be as strong as when children attempt to understand and adapt to their parents' own bitterness and prejudices.

One evening in the counseling room after a crusade, two sis- ters slowly poured out their story to a counselor. "I used to live with my dad," said one. "Now I live with my mom. My dad and her dad are brothers. Mom divorced my dad and married my sister's dad, but now they're divorcing too, so it's just easier to live with mom."

When the counselor proceeded to sympathize and soothe the children, the oldest replied, "Oh, it's no big deal. Mom says that she only married my uncle to hurt my dad because he divorced her. She didn't really love him; she just wanted to get even."

The counselor was stunned by the child's easy acceptance of the mother's disturbing behavior. Mom was teaching those chil- dren that bitterness and vengeance are the way to feel good about your situation. This atmosphere told them that there was no such thing as forgiving love. For them, what should have been a haven of rest was a home of confusion.

Ours is a society of public anger. Demonstrations, strikes, and lawsuits dominate the local and national news. Children look into the eyes of their parents to see their reaction to all this and to learn how to deal with such emotions as anger. Just how easily we teach this was brought home to me while my family was vacation- ing with some good friends, the Whites.

The Whites had just purchased a restaurant franchise, and the opening was scheduled while they were on vacation. One day, Mr. White received a phone call saying there was a problem. It seems that another outlet in the same chain was also trying to open in a nearby town, but didn't have the chairs they needed. Without consulting Mr. White, they had sent a truck to his restaurant and convinced the manager to let them borrow his chairs, using the name of the restaurant chain owner as leverage.

We were all sitting in the car as Mr. White told the story. At first, everyone was silent. Finally the Whites' son Jason chimed in. "Aren't you mad at that guy, Dad? What are you going to do to him?" Visions of lawsuits went through my head, too.

Mr. White with great wisdom replied, "I'm upset, yes. But I can't just start reacting until I get *all* the facts." His wife nodded in agreement.

As it turned out, the Whites' restaurant opened on time after all, and the misunderstanding was cleared up. Later, Mr. White told me, "I really wanted to be mad, but all I could think of at that moment was that my boys were sitting behind me expecting a reaction. And I decided that I had to respond properly."

The other link found between affection in the home and healthy relationships as adults is *attachment*. Kids with affectionate parents who are obviously strongly attached to each other develop a stronger sense of internal security. This enables them to engage with other people in social relationships, instead of withdrawing.

Sometimes the sense of attachment is so lacking in the home that teenagers will do all they can to be somewhere else. Do you ever wonder why your child always wants to go to someone else's house or is never at home? Perhaps he or she is escaping from the pressure of your home, seeking comfort and just plain fun in another family.

I know of one home where teens are coming and going every afternoon and evening. "It gets noisy," says Mom, "but I know where they are and what they're doing and who they're doing it with. And even if my own children don't tell me what is going on, their friends usually fill me in. So I cheerfully set another plate for dinner or answer the doorbell when it rings."

Because this home is one where anyone and everyone is loved and accepted for who they are, it is one where teens flock. Because it is run by emotionally healthy adults, it attracts teens in search of emotional health.

An Atmosphere of Peace and Safety

In a survey of teens I conducted, the number one thing they said they would like to change in their home is their parents fighting with each other. Very simply, it scares them. The second change they said they would make had to do with the arguing between them and their parents.

Remember, home is the "safe place," the "womb," a place of protection from the confusion of the outside world. When arguments rule the home, all of those securities are threatened. When you ask a child what the arguments in the home are about, they often don't remember, but they remember the threat to their sense of security that the arguments pose.

Arguments between children and their parents often arise over attitudes in the children that their parents think are "silly." Let's face it—children do come up with some silly ideas, but that's the fun of having a youthful imagination. Parents seem to enjoy kids' creativity when they express new ideas with which the parents agree. But when they disagree, parents tend to dismiss the kids' ideas. "It's not that big a deal." "That's silly; just forget it." Or, "I don't know why you're upset; you'll be fine." In this atmosphere, children develop the attitude that it's not worth talking to their folks; they either don't understand or they don't really care.

"Of course, I care," you want to scream. "I give every ounce of my energy for this family." But the interactions in many homes remind me of the two porcupines who found themselves out in the cold one night. They desperately needed each other's warmth, but every time they tried to get together they would needle each other!

If we were to examine the anatomy of an argument, we would discover that each of the parties wants his or her own way. The quarrel is fueled by a war of wills. Again, we can learn from the business world here. In the world of negotiating business deals there is what is called the "win-win" deal. Discussion is volleyed back and forth until both parties feel they have benefited from the final decision.

This can work in families, too. Just remember, parents: In order for a "win-win" conversation to occur, both parties must understand that there will have to be some give and take.

Steven Covey summarizes the single most important principle he has learned in relationships as *"Seek first to understand, then to be understood."*[1] To do otherwise is like making the diagnosis without first examining the patient.

When you as a parent notice that most conversations with your kids are becoming arguments, it is time to reevaluate the communication in your home. Do you always have to have your way, or are you open-minded enough to see their point of view? Do you find yourself saying things like, "Because I said so!" "I don't want to hear it!" "That's just the way it is!"? All such statements fuel anger and resentment.

Taking the time to listen objectively does not have to involve a compromise of your values, nor does it endanger the level of authority in the home. I sometimes think that James may have been speaking of family discussions when he said, "The wrath of man does not produce the righteousness of God" (James 1:20).

What causes conflict? It may not always be the big things like curfew and parties. It may just be the clash of opinions or a lack of sensitivity that sets up barriers to communication. Consider these pairs of statements:

"I'm still hungry" . . . "You can't be hungry. We just ate an hour ago."

"I don't like this dress" . . . "Of course, you like it. It's perfect for you."

"School was so boring today" . . . "It was probably
very interesting, but you didn't pay attention."

Each of these pairs of statements says, "You're wrong; I'm
right" and "Your opinions are false; mine are true."

Or consider your conversation when there are hurt feelings.
Genuine feelings of empathy, no matter how small the hurt, are
always met with relieved acceptance. The next step can then be
encouragement to go on, but we cannot skip the healing step. We
often have our emotional first aid backward—we encourage first
and hope that this will bring healing and relief. Instead, we must
first do something about the problem at hand. Do your children
need to know you love them? Tell them! Do you need to apolo-
gize? Make your confession! Have they just made a mess of something? Help them clean it up! Then you can lead them on to the
next set of challenges with confidence.

Dr. Charles Stanley advises, "A noncommunicative parent
has the potential to destroy the self-esteem of kids." Dr. Stanley
believes that if noncommunication keeps a person from fulfilling
a God-given responsibility as a parent, it is nothing less than sin.[2]

Toward Better Communication

Establishing an atmosphere of peace rather than conflict
might well begin with what *not* to do. I'm thinking especially of
using guilt to change a child's behavior or opinion. There is no
such thing as positive guilt. The Scripture teaches repentance;
that is, a change of heart. It does not teach guilt, which is carrying around the burden of sin. Don't lay a guilt trip on your child
such as "How could you embarrass me like that?" "You hurt me so
badly!" Grow up, parent! God doesn't treat us like that, and we
certainly shouldn't pass it on to our kids.

If a child cannot experience forgiveness at home, where will
he ever find it in the world? If she does not learn it from her parents, her dearest friends, who will teach it to her? It is much easier
for you to take on hurt feelings than it is for an already emotionally bruised child to do so. Be careful—your satisfaction in "winning" arguments could make your child feel like a loser. Of course

we have to teach our children responsibility, but guilt is no way to go about it.

We must also show our children compassion. Whoever said "Sticks and stones may break my bones, but words will never hurt me" was not looking at life through the eyes of a child. Certainly they are hurt by statements such as, "You act so dumb sometimes." "That was a stupid thing to do." "You're a selfish brat." Or my favorite statement, one that I hear in airports, at church, and other public places: "Stop acting like a child!" The child innocently stares at his mother with the thought, "I *am* a child. How else can I act?" Words like these not only hurt at the moment; they may turn out to be self-fulfilling prophecies.

Beware of the trap of absolutes such as "always" and "never." With these words you immediately set yourself up for correction and an ensuing quarrel.

Sometimes it's hard to say what we would like to say in the heat of a disagreement. If all else fails, put your instructions in a note and add a word of praise and encouragement. In this way you can carefully think out what you want to say.

In one of the "Family Circus" cartoons, dad is shown sitting in his chair reading the paper while Billy sits at his feet talking. Billy looks at dad and says, "Daddy, listen to me with your eyes!" The point is that *attentive listening is the foundation of all effective talking or communication.*

Keep in mind that what seems insignificant to you may loom large in the mind of a growing child. Dr. Ward Walker, dean of spiritual affairs at East Texas Baptist University, gave me some good advice as a young father: "Jay, the way to get your kids off your back is to put them in your heart. Establish a friendship with them and work at becoming best friends."

Because of their love and respect for you, your children's perception of how you sympathize with their feelings directly affects their opinion of themselves and, consequently, their behavior.

The Appetites That Drive Your Home

What are your appetites? What is it that drives you, that motivates you? When your children think of mom and dad's priorities, what do they feel you place the most value in day in and day out? A "healthy appetite"—godly motivations—are crucial to making your home a taste of heaven.

More than Money

God used a committed father in our church recently to move my heart regarding the value of motivation that is higher than materialism. He was trying to decide whether to accept a significant promotion at work that involved a move. On the one hand, the promotion offered more money, more prestige, and more job security. On the other hand, it meant less time for his children, leaving behind a growing Sunday school class he was teaching, resigning from his responsibility as a deacon in his church, and uprooting his family.

He told me that even as he began praying, he knew God was leading him to reject the lucrative offer. In the end, that's just what he did. What was so interesting was that he never once seemed to feel regret of any kind. I believe with all my heart it was because his criteria for the decision had been set long before: He had developed a healthy appetite for what really counts.

Bowing down at the golden calf of materialism sends a clear message of priorities to our children. This man sent a different message. His children learned that *life is not about what we possess, but what possesses us.*

The Good vs. the Best

We can give our kids the best in material gain as long we do not teach that material gain is the best. Even Socrates, the Greek philosopher, knew better than many Christian families when he said, "Fellow citizens, why do you turn and scrape every stone to gather wealth and take so little care of your children, to whom one day you must relinquish it all?" Parents who are driven by the need for status, by a passion for a new car, a larger house, or designer clothing may send a message that self-worth is built upon these things rather than upon faith in God, wisdom, and godly character.

In her book *Meeting God at Every Turn,* Catherine Marshall gives a wonderful account of the reality of her mother's faith in a chapter called "Mother Never Thought We Were Poor." She writes that, in their home, faith was as real as anyone else's bank account. It was "as real as the mountain air we breathed and the nourishing bread she baked, as solid as the gold in Fort Knox. Mother's family bank account was her faith in the Lord, her absolute trust that the promise 'give and it shall be given unto you' was as eternal as the mountains around us."[3]

The best things in life are not things.

Making Time a Priority

Michael Pritchard, a former juvenile probation officer, talked with more than twenty thousand teenagers across the country while taping a Public Broadcasting System special called "The Power of Choice." He concluded that the number one thing kids want is to spend more time with their parents. In second place is to know that their moms and dads want to spend time with them. Pritchard claims that thousands of teens today have a disease he calls "malnutrition of the spirit." In the end, we give them many of the things we never had, but we fail to give them the love and energy that we have.

I heard of a young man who came home from school depressed and feeling like a failure. His moping was so obvious that his father came upstairs to cheer him up. "I tell you what, son. Let's just you and me spend the day together tomorrow. We'll go fishing." The boy was elated. The day of quiet sharing was a healing balm for his ego, and it put the fight back into his spirit. This was a memory of his dad he would never forget.

Later that night the boy sat thinking about the great respect he felt for his dad. He decided to glance through his father's journal to learn more about what he thought. Imagine this young man's disillusionment when he read, on the page for that day, this notation: "Today was a wasted day. No phone calls. No new contacts. No sales. Spent the whole day fishing with my son."

Parents, we are going to have to schedule our lives to meet the needs of our kids. Appointments and responsibilities can and often must be rescheduled to accomplish your number one role of life: parenting. We, and no one else, have the task of guiding our children from childhood to adulthood, from dependence to independence, from foolishness to responsibility.

The question of time is relative to the urgency of the task. It is like the commercial for the oil and air filters for our cars: "You can pay me now or you can pay me later. Spend a few extra dollars now or hundreds when it's too late." Likewise, parents can spend time with their children now, or spend time lamenting the loss of their children later.

Charles Hummel, author of *The Tyranny of the Urgent*, writes this about time with family: "Important things tend to get pushed out of the way in deference to what is immediately urgent and pressing."[4] The tyranny of the urgent is a prescription for financial failure in the business world and for personal disaster in the family.

Teaching Through Actions

One evening, looking up at a beautiful starlit sky, my daughters and I talked about the splendor of the stars. "Girls, look!" I exclaimed. "It's a falling star!" We all oohed and aahed over the spectacular sight.

Later I thought about that scene. Here were thousands of stars visible to the naked eye, each one taking its place in the heavens as they have through the ages, yet the one that caught our attention was the falling star.

The same holds true of what we see as "falling" heroes—including religious leaders. For every one that the media oohs and aahs over, we must remind ourselves and those around us of the thousands standing faithfully at their post, serving the Lord with all diligence.

Still, it is very disturbing to all of us when it happens, not only because of the bad testimony for the Lord's sake, but also because of the great disappointment that we feel when it is someone whom we trusted, loved, and admired. Try to imagine for a moment the feeling you had when you first heard of a minister you respected who had been caught in an affair or some other type of indiscretion. Now multiply that pain a hundredfold, and you have some idea of how a child feels when it happens within her own family. It is a betrayal of trust and of all the child holds dear. It can be devastating.

An Example of Self-Control

The example we offer to teens must be one of self-control. We cannot expect them to do any more or less than we do. Martin Luther said, "You can't keep the birds from flying over your head, but you can keep them from building a nest in your hair!"

Temptations come. We have decisions to make in life, and we are affected by the things we see and hear. By grace we are given the power to choose those things that will occupy our minds and determine our morality. It is up to us to deal with the tempting desire or thought before it becomes sin. We have the example of Jesus to encourage us: "For we do not have a High Priest who cannot sympathize with our weaknesses, but was in all points tempted as we are, yet without sin" (Heb. 4:15).

While we are teaching control, we must live control. That begins by avoiding temptation. I am amazed at the number of men who flirt with the idea of an office romance. Never really intending to do anything about it, they continue to play the game because it feeds their ego.

I meet very few men who tell me, "I just decided to go out and have an affair." Instead, they speak in shame of the offhand flirting that they never intended to follow through on but which got out of hand. Everywhere I preach I tell women, "Don't be flattered that a man is willing to use you. Just because your husband doesn't compliment you, or is no longer the Prince Charming of your dreams, does not mean that the man who wants to use you only for your body will compliment you or stay around long enough to care."

The standard is simple for you and your children: Don't be alone with anyone you are sexually attracted to. God offers help for coping with both the desires of the body and the thoughts of the mind, which really are the same. In Romans 12:1–2 He tells us to *renew* the mind—that is, to exchange evil thoughts for good ones. Feed yourself Scripture and your temptations will starve to death.

The Power of Example

Albert Schweitzer said, "Example is not a way to teach; it is the only way to teach." The Women's Sports Foundation provides a positive illustration of this truth in reporting that 70 percent of young girls who participate in sports have parents who are involved in sporting activities as well.

Your example sets the rules. My wife and I remind our girls over and over—it is not whether you are "old enough" to hear the music or see the video or movie or attend the event. It is a decision based on what you want to put in your mind, who you want to be around, and what kind of situations you want to be faced with. If, however, I set up a different standard of what is acceptable for myself than I do for my children, I send them the opposite message. While I am certainly old enough for any entertainment, I find that much of it is not suitable to the type of life I want to lead or the images I want to remain in my mind.

We want our actions to teach our children to trust in God and to fight the evil that comes against them. For example, many of today's families are beset by financial problems. Instead of hiding out of pride or taking your anger out on the family, bring them together in planning, working, and praying for a solution. They will feel more stress because of your coverup than they will feel if you are leading the way in trusting God to meet your needs.

We must communicate to them that our faith lies not in the temporal but in the eternal, and that conviction must be backed up by our actions both in day-to-day activities and in our relationship to the Lord. Kids need models more than they need critics. The responsibility for what goes on in our homes when the curtain is drawn is not to be taken lightly.

Mother Teresa said, "Love begins at home. It is not how much we do, but how much love we put in the action that we do."

10

Breaking the Cycle of Pain

Confronting Family Dysfunctions

$P_{okazukha}$ is an old Russian word that means "to show." The people of the Soviet Union adapted the word to their living situation in 1980 when the Olympic Games were held in Moscow. Prior to the event, entire streets were repaved and planted with trees and hundreds of city blocks were freshly painted overnight to impress foreign guests.

Citizens cried out against the work, claiming it was *pokazukha*—mere deception. While the outside of the homes looked like model housing, inside the basements were flooded with stagnant water, the plumbing was in disrepair, and there was no heat. Any favorable impression on the outsiders was overshadowed by the rage of those living inside.[1]

Pain on the Inside?

I am afraid that too many families are also whitewashed on the outside for approval's sake; inside they are decaying and in need of repair. Sadly, the exterior primping continues while inside there are dreary cycles of pain, and children are drowning in the stagnant backwash of their parents' own hypocrisy.

I urge parents to take an inventory of their strengths and weaknesses and to deal with unfinished emotional business and pain from the past. Beware of inconsistencies in your own character and your decision-making process. An honest and open look at your own childhood and teen years may reveal much about why you make the kind of parental decisions you do.

Failing to make such a personal inventory can perpetuate several kinds of cycles.

The Cycle of Abuse

It is not difficult to recognize the active abuse that occurs through physical, verbal, or sexual aggression, but we often forget that we can also abuse our kids by ignoring and neglecting them. Whether the abuse is emotional, sexual, or physical, it must be interrupted and dealt with before you take another step with your own children.

I myself was a victim of physical, emotional, and sexual abuse as a child. I have never been tempted to physically or sexually abuse my own children, but it took me some time to realize that I could also be abusive with the words I used. For example, I had been called "stupid" and put down verbally so often that harsh words came out of my mouth any time I felt the situation with my own children was not under my control. I believed I was being a good disciplinarian. In fact I was only acting out the verbal abuse of my own childhood. Once I understood what was going on, I was able to be more sensitive and work at carefully calculating my conversation with my children. You, too, may need to make a conscientious effort to break a chain of abuse, whether verbal or otherwise.

Recently someone coined the phrase "emotional incest" to describe one way parents can abuse their children emotionally. Although the term is new, the abuse that it describes has been going on for generations. The parent becomes unable to deal with the stress of the home and/or of the past, so he or she forms an "incestual" link with the child, unloading both his or her emotional needs and parental responsibility on the child. It just isn't fair. Parents must instead learn to trust God to bear their pain, moving out of the syndrome and breaking the cycle.

If you want to raise emotionally healthy children, you must be healthy yourself. Your kids are not mature enough to shoulder

your neuroses. For their sakes, if not your own, seek help immediately if you feel you can no longer function as a spouse or parent.

Living Through the Child

A second and little-recognized cycle is the pain created
when a parent tries to live vicariously through a child. For example, the mother who was always overweight or never dated
wants her daughter to look perfect and go to every social event
that she never had the chance to attend. The father who never
made it on the football team desperately wants his son to make it,
so he pushes his son to participate in sports regardless of the son's
ability or wishes.

The parent who was a popular teenager may insist that her
own child be as popular. In truth, the teen may be shy or quiet or
of a totally different personality. This produces unfair pressure on
the child and is not healthy for the parents.

Likewise, the parent who was a promiscuous teen may accuse
or be constantly suspicious, setting up a clash in further commu-
nications. Many parents continue to push their children into lives
they themselves would have liked to lead. Parents should see this
as unfinished emotional business which has to be dealt with before they can be whole persons and effective parents.

Beware of dealing with your pain by living vicariously
through your teen. He has his own life and his own challenges and
doesn't need the leftovers of an unfinished agenda from your own
background.

The Cycle of Defeatism

A tragic cycle of pain is created by the parent who learned to
be a victim as a child and then "wills" defeatism to his own children. On the conscious level we try to teach our children survival
skills that will carry them through difficult times. They must learn
how to survive when a job falls through, finances look bleak, or
the doctor's report leaves them fearful. Yet past experiences of
learned defeatism can cause us to fail to live up to these lessons

ourselves. Thus we perpetuate the cycle in our children by example, if not by our words.

I have found that the Lord often tests me in the very face of my own kids. Our children will learn far more about "taking the tests" from watching us than from listening to us.

Single parents must be especially careful at this point. They may have felt victimized by an ex-spouse, continuing to harbor bitterness. Unless they make a conscious effort to break the cycle, they can damage their children by venting their angry feelings on them, thus teaching them to be victims, too.

In my life it worked like this. I was a victim for thirteen years. Many things happened that weren't fair or right, but I had absolutely no control over them. My dad was drowning himself in alcohol, and he took us with him. It wasn't my fault. I wasn't the only one to ever experience this type of pain or abuse, and I didn't know how to cope.

In response, I exchanged the role of a victim for that of a villain. I knew what was right, but I couldn't seem to put it together for myself. Since every villain needs a victim, I continued the cycle by making victims of those around me.

Now I am a victor. I had to stop viewing those who hurt me through the blurred vision of my tears and begin to see them with the clarity of God's perspective. I had to decide that I was not going to allow toxic parents or personalities to poison the well that I had to drink from for the rest of my life and which I would leave as a heritage for my children to drink from. I realized that I was crucifying my today between the thief of yesterday and the thief of "I'll get help tomorrow."

New Help for Breaking Old Cycles

Second Corinthians 5:17 has been a therapeutic verse for me personally in breaking the cycles of pain. Paul said, "If anyone is in Christ, he is a new creation; old things have passed away; behold, all things have become new."

This passage offers healing for the past and power for the present. It implies three things.

1. A *new position*. In Christ I am a part of a new family. I am in the family of God.

2. A *new personality*. I don't have to be a cheap imitation of a screamer or a hysterical parent with out-of-control emotions. People use as an excuse, "My mother was this way." It is a sin to say, "I can't help it." You have Christ in you, the hope of glory. Ask yourself, Why am I the way I am when I could be the way Christ wants me to be?

3. A *new potential*. I realize that, if I want to, I can break free from the bondage and begin again.

For many years the Christian community has pictured the ideal family like a Norman Rockwell painting, with all its simple, old-fashioned purity. However, it is becoming painfully obvious that many modern families more closely resemble the work of Picasso during his Cubist period.

In Picasso's Cubist work, faces are not completely in focus and many of the lines and contours do not quite meet. Isn't that a fair description of many homes? Our home life may never attain the virginal simplicity we once dreamed of, but if we will learn to shake off the dust of past failures, God can truly work miracles in my family and in yours.

I strongly urge you as a parent to "heal thyself" of the pain of your past, so you can break the cycle of pain and not pass it on to the children God has placed under your care.

Family Analysis

1. What were the strengths and weaknesses of your family when you were growing up?
2. Were any of these characteristics present in your family?

Addictions:

☐ alcoholism   ☐ gambling addiction

☐ drug addiction   ☐ sexual addiction

☐ workaholism   ☐ success or money addiction

☐ eating disorder   ☐ other addiction _____

Other dysfunctional characteristics:

☐ divorce   ☐ domineering father/
                               passive mother

☐ neglect   ☐ domineering mother/
                               passive father

☐ sexual abuse   ☐ psychosomatic illness

☐ verbal abuse   ☐ loss of memory

☐ emotional abuse   ☐ constant tension/anxiety

☐ physical abuse   ☐ depression

☐ "smothering" by parent   ☐ other _____

3. Describe your relationship with your father (pros and cons).
4. Describe your relationship with your mother (pros and cons).
5. Describe your relationship with each of your siblings (pros and cons).
6. Describe how these relationships affected you regarding:
   a. Healthy self-esteem vs. shame.
   b. Experiencing forgiveness vs. guilt.
   c. Expressing forgiveness vs. being condemning and critical of others.

d. Love vs. hate.

e. Accurate perceptions vs. black-and-white perspectives of people or situations.

f. The ability to set limits vs. being overly responsible.

g. Being responsible for your behavior vs. irresponsibility.

h. Good bonding in relationships vs. loneliness.

i. Ability to have your own opinions, feelings, and decisions vs. being a puppet or people pleaser.

j. Ability to have fun vs. being stiff or depressed.

k. Ability to talk, feel, and trust vs. repressed emotions/explosions of anger.

7. What strengths have been built into your life as a result of your family background?

8. What weaknesses or needs have developed in your life as a result of your family background?

9. How do the strengths and weaknesses affect your leadership/relationships in your present family? (How do you respond when people dominate, withdraw, disagree, fawn over you, etc?)

10. What have you learned about yourself and your family from this analysis?

11. How can you be better prepared to function in your family in view of what you have learned about yourself?

11

Friendly Fire

Internal Problems That Could Sabotage Your Family

In 1991, perhaps as never before, Americans bowed their knees before the Lord, asking with one heart for His divine intervention in the Persian Gulf War. Those who rarely thought of or mentioned the name of God were now giving Him praise as we watched the awesome display of American weaponry. Television shows ran for hours, some continuously, explaining battle plans, interviewing specialists, showing us reports from the actual fighting. Most of us were strengthened and encouraged by the incredible technology that seemed to make us invincible.

Then, on Wednesday, January 30, an Air Force A-10 fighter aimed a heat-seeking Maverick missile at an Iraqi tank. Heat radiating from a Marine light armored vehicle attracted the missile's homing device instead, and an instrument of destruction intended for the enemy went astray—seven American soldiers lay dead in the sand.

What should have been the ultimate in protection became the supreme destroyer. Our own soldiers were dead, not because of the enemy's power, but because of friendly fire.

On the home front, nothing seems sadder than the stories we read of a brother killing his brother when a gun accidentally fires during cleaning. We grieve at the death of any child, but it seems to be a double tragedy when a father backs out of the driveway onto his own child.

As gruesome as these stores are, this same danger is occurring on a daily basis in the spiritual lives of our children. In this case it is not peer pressure nor the school environment nor the media that are killing our children. The killer consists of forces in the home itself.

In this chapter I want to confront this problem on two main fronts—sibling rivalry and miscommunication.

The Problem of Sibling Rivalry

Much of today's popular comedy is centered around sibling rivalry. "The Simpsons" television show and the "Home Alone" movies are just two examples. Unfortunately, such portrayals only confirm the kind of temperament that abounds in many homes today, both Christian and non-Christian.

The First Murder

It is interesting but sad to note that earth's first family was touched by such intense sibling rivalry that it resulted in the first murder—the death of Abel by the hand of Cain. In our own day the problem is more commonly reflected in our family talk. "Stop hitting me!" "You always ignore me!" "I wish you were dead." "I hate you!" These tragic yet familiar barbs are hurled carelessly at siblings, in even the "nicest" of families. As a parent, you have no doubt noticed how quickly these toxic feelings can contaminate the spirit of a family.

This combative attitude becomes even more complex with the prevalence of blended families and single-parent homes as the result of our continued high divorce rate. These are the verbal outcries of hurting youth from broken families with fractured self-esteem. "Why do I have to move and give up my room?" "It's not fair I have to leave my friends." "I don't want you to be my brother." "You'll never be my mother." You may not have all the answers, yet these are the young people you must now minister to as a parent.

Fortunately, God has addressed this difficult subject throughout the pages of the Bible, including the fascinating ac-count of prenatal sibling rivalry between the brothers Esau and

Jacob (Gen. 25:22–26). The same symptoms that appear in the story of Cain and Abel—jealousy, comparison, and resentment— are vividly echoed in the account of Joseph and his "blended" family. It is worth noting that Joseph's problem stemmed from parental favoritism, and the sad result was a severed relationship that could be repaired only by God's intervention.

The New Testament reveals the same tragic consequences in the parable of the prodigal son. This parable highlights the tension and envy of the "more responsible" elder brother toward the wayward, younger brother, to the point of breaking fellowship with the father.

Even in the life of the Lord Jesus, this problem surfaced. Jesus was the firstborn in His family, and although we never read of His being jealous or angry, the Scripture hints at a strained relationship on the part of His brothers and sisters during the years of His ministry (see John 7:5).

It is no wonder that the psalmist wrote, "Behold, how good and how pleasant it is for brethren to dwell together in unity" (Ps. 133:1).

The Power of Sibling Relationships

One of the most effective bridges that you can build with your child is the bridge between him and his siblings. One of the most helpful lessons that I have ever communicated to my own children has been the long-range principle that long after they are out on their own, for years down the road, it is not uncommon to turn to a brother or sister for security and emotional support throughout life. It is as though we are connected with super glue; that is, we are stuck with each other for the rest of our years. However, the actions, words, and reactions of today can poison the well for tomorrow.

Solomon, the wisest man ever to live, describes it well: "A friend loves at all times, and a brother is born for adversity" (Prov. 17:17). This is also echoed in the old adage, "A brother is like ivy: the greater the ruin, the closer it clings." As normal as family bickering may sometimes seem, it must nevertheless be labeled for

what it is—sin against God and against the family—and dealt
with as such.

Prescription for Sibling Rivalry

As a parent, you can be God's person standing in the gap to
help cement these cracks in the temperament and emotions of
your kids.

Here are nine principles to keep in mind when dealing with
this problem.

**1. Distinguish between harmful sibling rivalry and healthy
give-and-take.** Not all sibling rivalry should be discouraged, because it can be the means of working out conflicts within the family. Remember that the home is often a classroom for learning to
verbalize emotions and hurt feelings. How many marriages have
ended and careers destroyed because adults never learned the
skills of cooperation, communication, and dealing with conflict as
a young person? However, always draw the line at hateful speech
or vengeful attitudes.

2. Destructive sibling rivalry can be overcome. Because it is
sin, it can be dealt with as such—repented of, replaced with new
goals, both emotionally and spiritually. Our children must understand that jealousy and pride are sins against God, not just idle
words or harmless feelings. By teaching them this, we teach them
about being rightly related to God and to others through learning
to control self. "Let nothing be done through selfish ambition or
conceit, but in lowliness of mind let each esteem others better
than himself" (Phil. 2:3).

3. Don't "provoke children to wrath" through favoritism.
Sibling rivalry is naturally increased in the home where favoritism
is shown, or when a child is constantly compared with siblings, as
we discussed in the case of Joseph.

**4. Spend time daily with each child, building up his self-
esteem.** Remember that in spite of hectic schedules your child is
worth this individual attention. Often sibling rivalry is a cry on
the part of the teen to be appreciated and loved for himself.

5. Remember that positive parents encourage positive kids. "Yes, you are different from your sister. That's the way God planned it. Let's make a list of things *you* like to do, of *your* goals and strengths. Together we can come up with a plan to meet those goals."

6. Help children understand why destructive sibling rivalry is sin. "Out of the same mouth proceed blessing and cursing. My brethren, these things ought not to be so" (James 3:10).

7. Explain that two people can disagree without being disagreeable. By doing so, you can enable your children to learn social skills as well as family skills. They will be confronted with conflict and competition the rest of their lives. What better way to learn than with the family who loves them!

8. Help kids understand the barrier in their relationship with God that disharmony creates. Few young people (or adults for that matter) understand that harsh, hateful relationships create a barrier in their relationship with God—not just with each other. This is clearly indicated by the apostle John:

> He who says he is in the light, and hates his brother, is in darkness until now. He who loves his brother abides in the light, and there is no cause for stumbling in him. But he who hates his brother is in darkness and walks in darkness, and does no know where he is going, because the darkness has blinded his eyes.
>
> 1 John 2:9–11

9. Help your children to understand the root of their rivalry. Why do they feel and act as they do? Could it be an attitude problem on their part? Using the biblical accounts of Jacob and Esau, Joseph and his brothers, Cain and Abel, etc., teach weekly studies with practical application and food for thought. Then give time for discussion and for decision.

A biblical perspective will allow them to see their own mistakes in the lives of others. It also enables them to channel their feelings into positive growth. Remember that the powerful Word of God never returns void. *You are not looking for immediate results; you are laying the foundation for growth, for growing into a responsible, caring person who is able to resolve conflict and endure disappointment.*

Emphasize to your children that *they* are responsible for controlling their attitudes and relationships with each other. Former high school principal Joe Clark, subject of the 1989 film *Lean on Me*, stated, "The responsibility for your condition is in your own hands. Self-responsibility is the brick and mortar of success."

The Friendly Fire of Poor Leadership in the Home

When asked to speak concerning leadership, General Norman Schwarzkopf gave eleven principles that surprisingly parallel the requirements of good leadership in the home. Or perhaps it's not surprising, since there are a number of homes that resemble a battleground! Motivating, organizing, and leading thousands of soldiers and commanders could be done through sheer authority, although not very effectively. The following guidelines from the hero of the Gulf War are far better.[1]

Toward More Effective Leadership

1. You must have clear goals. During the war, the goal was easily understood: "Get the Iraqis out of Kuwait." Each family must also have goals that everyone understands, written and discussed in easily understood language.

2. Give yourself a clear agenda. General Schwarzkopf suggests that every day you write down the five most important things to accomplish that day. A "to do" list has become essential to the lives of men and women both inside and outside the home. What a wonderful way to be *intentional* about the influence you will have on a child today.

3. Let people know where they stand. The "grades" you give the people who report to you must reflect reality. Don't shield kids from every discouragement. Instead, work with them to receive the courage to face the need for improvement.

4. What's broken, fix now. Problems that aren't dealt with lead to other problems. Enough said.

5. No repainting the flagpole. Make sure all the work that is being done is essential to the organization.

6. Set high standards. People generally won't perform above your expectations, so it's important to expect a lot. As parents, this should not mean setting achievement standards alone, but high moral standards as well.

7. Lay the concept out, but let your people execute it. Give them the ideas, then step back and allow them to do their own work.

8. People come to work to succeed. Nobody comes to work to fail. No child wants to be a failure. Enable him or her to be a success.

9. Never lie, ever. During the war, someone suggested that the Allies use "disinformation" to mislead the Iraqis through the use of our own media, such as CNN, which they were monitoring and watching. General Schwarzkopf vetoed the idea, because he felt it would undermine the military leadership's credibility with the American public. If you can lie for any reason, then the child feels he or she can lie when it seems necessary.

10. When in charge, take command. The best policy is to decide, monitor the results, and change course if necessary. Making a mistake as a parent does not make you a failure or diminish you in the eyes of your children. What they are really interested in is how you face your own mistakes.

11. Do what is right. "The truth of the matter," says Schwarzkopf, "is that you always know the right thing to do. The hard part is doing it."

These basic leadership qualities all rely on the attainment of the first one: You must have clear goals. Everyone must understand what is expected, what we believe, where we stand on issues, and how our family operates.

Keeping Standards in Perspective

A mother approached me one evening after a service. She was distraught and in tears, so I agreed to talk and pray with her about her daughter. After the first few minutes of the conversation, I began to quit listening. She wanted me to talk to her daughter about her room. It seems it was always a mess and she feared that this indicated that her daughter's behavior was out of control.

I calmly asked, "Does your daughter disobey you in other ways? Is she rebellious?"

"No," said the mother. "You've got to talk to her."

I looked this woman in the eyes with as much seriousness as I could muster and told her, "Ma'am, go home and get on your knees and thank God for this girl and leave her alone about her room."

Every day I hear of parents with broken hearts over the loss of a child through drug use, a pregnant girl who has run away, a rebellious son who dominates the home with his anger. Here was this mother, upset enough over a messy room to speak to a minister, yet too caught up in herself to be grateful for clean morals. She was telling her daughter that she would never live up to her standards, that she would never be good enough.

"It's never enough for him," John tells me, speaking of his father. "He's never happy."

Mary cries, "I just wanted to be loved for who I am instead of who they say I should be. Now I'm in trouble."

Too often we attack the person when all we really mean to do is offer correction. "That's a dumb thing to do!" could be replaced with "I think we can find a better way." "What a pig you are!" might be better received as "It's time to clean up this mess of a room."

After all, disorganized school work is not actually a character flaw; it is behavior in need of modification. Try to channel your frustration into the situation rather than the person. The focus should not be on the wrong but on the *cause* behind the wrong.

The family has enough enemies from without. Let's not waste our ammunition on friendly fire, allowing our own actions and attitudes to attack the family from within.

12

Reaching for the Stars

How to Motivate Your Kids

It was with great delight that I read the account of W. Phillip Keller's childhood memories in *Heroes:*

> The constant impression that came to me as a small lad was that Dad, Mother, and God were all caught up in an exciting adventure together. Life was full of fresh advances. It abounded with new endeavors. New frontiers were being opened with faith and optimism.[1]

There, I think, is the key to it all—optimism. The twenty-first-century American family needs very little of the "No, you can't," but a whole lot of, "Let us go forward together with the Lord." Keller goes on to say, "The grace of God, the touch of the Master's hand, the gentle influence of God's gracious Spirit were so apparent in [father's] character and conduct that for me as a growing youth it was an ongoing miracle. He was my hero!"[2]

The home—the womb of the child's future—is that place where emotional fences are mended, where dreams are encouraged, where spirits are taught to soar, and where the reality of God is manifested. The attitude at home can truly be, "Be yourself," but it should also be, "Be better."

Somehow, we must teach our kids that they can be genuine, that they can be honest; they don't have to be perfect. But if perfection is an illusion, striving for excellence must be a very real way of life. The sheer delight of enjoying one another's company, encouraging and uplifting each other—this is the home where children grow into well-adjusted adults. Success is not defined by how much you do together, but by living each day to the fullest potential as a family.

Foundations of Motivation

Our children's motivation can be built on four foundation stones.

God Can Do It

If this essential is not solidly implanted in the heart, all else is of no avail. Great strength can be added to one's faith by rehearsing the wondrous deeds of God through the Scripture. Easily recalled stories of the Bible learned from childhood should be played over and over in the theater of the mind, as should answers to prayer in the lives of family members, friends, and other testimonies.

The apostle Paul praised "Him who is able to do exceedingly abundantly above all that we ask or think" (Eph. 3:20). (Which, I might add, is saying a great deal since children can certainly imagine some amazing things!)

God Can Do It Through Me

Yes, me! If His requirement is a heart of faith, then it will happen through me. In the mind's eye, the vision can be seen as reality. There is great power in believing.

As Samuel sought the one whom God had chosen to be the next king over Israel, God said, "Do not look at his appearance or at his physical stature. . . . For the Lord does not see as man sees; for man looks at the outward appearance, but the Lord looks at the heart" (1 Sam. 16:7).

God Can Do It Through Me Now

Right now, while I am still learning and growing, God can use me to accomplish His will. Young people are always tempted to think, "When I am older . . . ," "When I am better able . . . ," "If only I could. . . ." Assist your child in visualizing the finished goal and continually keeping it before him. Teens must grasp the fact that God is even now thinking of them, planning for them, listening to their needs, and working things together for a future of hope.

"'For I know the thoughts that I think toward you,' says the LORD, 'thoughts of peace and not of evil, to give you a future and a hope'" (Jer. 29:11).

God Is Listening to Me

Right now, God is listening to the words of my mouth and the meditations of my heart in order to meet my needs and prepare my path. Nothing could be more encouraging, more satisfying, more strengthening, more helpful to the self-esteem of teenagers than to know that right now the Creator of the universe leans out of heaven and attunes His ears attentively to their every thought.

"'Then you will call upon Me and go and pray to Me, and I will listen to you'" (Jer. 29:12).

Helping Them to Find the Path

We motivate our kids by loving them unconditionally and completely while assisting them in finding the shortest distance and the straightest path between where they are and where they want to go.

While we assist in the navigation, we should understand that it is not our job to be the sole mapmaker. In the book *Learned Optimism*, Martin Seligman says that one of the most significant findings in the last thirty years of psychology is that individuals can choose the way they think: "Each of us carries a word in our heart. It is 'yes' or 'no.' Teaching your child optimism is as important as teaching him to work hard or to be truthful."[3] He also lists three factors of achievement—ability, desire, and optimism.

Helping Teens Find Their Talent

During this time when self-esteem is so easily bruised, it is urgent that the teen enter the adolescent years with some sort of skill that he or she can feel confident about. I cannot stress this enough. The hopeless feeling of "I'm not good at anything" is totally unnecessary. Everyone has been endowed by God with a special talent, ability, or gift. It is up to us to assist youth in uncovering the specialty and putting it into action. This essential is the beginning of self-esteem.

At our house, we call it "sampling." For example, the girls and I work out deals on starting new hobbies or ideas. We each pick one idea and give it a time limit. For instance, Christa wanted to increase her performing arts classes. I wanted her to use the extra time to take an evangelism class, but I really wanted it to be her idea. We prayed and prayed about it, but I told her she had the final call. She knew in her heart that balance would be the key and so she agreed to try both. We gave it a time limit of four weeks to see how this extra time would affect her school work. As of this writing, the jury is still out, but so far, so good!

Setting a time limit offers protection against feelings of failure and loss of self-worth. That's why it's helpful to call it "sampling"—by that we know that this is only a test to see if this is the best use of time and energy for the individual.

At the end of the time limit, encourage the child to ask some questions:

1. Is this something I enjoy doing?
2. Is it worth the time and energy that it may take away from other things, such as family time or school work?

3. Will I follow through in practice and attendance, which are absolutes?

4. Will this support our goals of making new friends, tackling challenges, and building tenacity?

5. Is this an opportunity for emotional, social, mental, and/or spiritual growth?

6. How can I measure all of the *good* goals against the *best?* Night after night of activities, even good ones, can overshadow the *best* goal of family time and growth together.

Success is not an accident nor is it merely luck or fate. The overwhelming excitement of victory, like that at the Olympic Games, can be carried out in our homes as we guide our children into small victories of their own. When "I can't" or "I don't think I can" evolves through much effort into "I did it!" there should be a joyous celebration throughout the family.

Helping Kids Set Goals

Don't leave your child's personality growth to chance. Personalities can and must be nurtured and developed, molded in character, and watered with truth. You are a real parent only when you provide for and prepare your child to be ready for life. Teaching your kids to set goals is part of the process.

John Maxwell, quoting a 1953 Yale University study, said that 3 percent of the graduating class had specific written goals for their lives. In 1975, researchers found that the 3 percent who wrote down their goals had accomplished more than the other 97 percent put together. Start small, but teach children to put their goals in writing.[4]

My older daughter loves goal setting. She seems to thrive on having that target to aim for. Her goals are practical and short term; in this way she sees results quickly and is able to build upon her confidence.

My younger daughter tends to write down dreams instead of short-term goals. Hers are the lofty "I wanna be's," and I have to work with her to fill in the blanks with the short-term goals that will enable her to reach for the stars.

Setting goals and attaining them lends energy to the increase of wisdom. Goals can be intimidating at first glance. To keep teens' motivation on track, assist in breaking down the goals into small bites. Each achievement then builds on the next, and excitement and pride grow.

This is also a time to assist your teen in conducting a self-survey to assess the realism of their goals. Here is a sample:

1. What is the one area that I want to change because I feel it would make the most difference in my life?
2. Do I have the ability to change it?
3. What do I need to do to accept about myself?
4. What do I see as weaknesses in my life?
5. What are my strengths?
6. What habit do I struggle with the most?
7. At what am I most consistent?

In a sense, *the end result is not the goal.* That is, it's the practice and growing while getting there that make the difference. As my good friend Zig Ziglar says, "It's not where you start, but where you finish."

When my daughter Melissa was just two months old, we were told that she needed surgery to close a valve in her heart. The only words I really heard the doctor say were, "Make sure you have a picture of her before she goes in . . . just in case." That newcomer into my life had become part of my soul, and I wept until it was over. She came through with flying colors, and we praised the Lord. At the age of two years, she had a simple surgery on her eyes. A few years later, we discovered she was hearing impaired and needed hearing aids.

Feeling that we were now on solid ground, we began to breathe easier when Melissa was suddenly struck with a seizure disorder that refused to respond to medication. It was a long year of struggle, emotionally and physically. A subsequent car accident left her with third-degree burns and a tight-fitting Jobst glove for healing. That trauma behind her, we discovered that she had scoliosis, a spinal disease that required her to wear a brace twenty-three hours a day.

Needless to say, all of this was quite a burden for this precious child, then only eleven years old. All of us in the family felt empathy for her, and it truly was a difficult period in our lives.

One evening as I sat studying in my room, I heard a "thump, thump, thump" on the stairs and the sound of tears. Rising from my chair, I met Melissa in the hall—dragging her brace, wearing her glove, and carrying her glasses, hearing aids, and medicine. "Honey, what's the matter?" I asked tenderly.

With a choked voice and a full heart she answered, "Daddy, I hate this stuff! I don't want to do this anymore! I won't do this anymore!" I listened quietly as she poured out her emotions—the embarrassment and discomfort of wearing the brace, the way the kids at school stared at her, the constant threat that a seizure might occur, and feeling like she had to be "repaired" every morning before she could leave for school.

By that time my own tears were flowing freely and I desperately prayed for wisdom. My compassion made me want to say, "Throw it all away. I love you just like you are," but God gave me more grace. "Melissa," I said, "I hate this brace, too!" and I slammed it down on the ground.

Wide-eyed and hopeful, she asked, "You do, Daddy?"

"Yes, honey, and I hate this medicine," I said, throwing it down next to the brace. I carefully *laid* the hearing aids down (those are expensive!) and took her into my arms for a long bear hug. But I knew I couldn't leave it there; we could not concede defeat. Holding on to her little shoulders and kneeling down to her eye level, I reassured her, "Melissa, I love you just the way you are . . . *but, I love you too much to leave you this way.*"

Now, several years later, I watch a young lady with a smile that lights up a room. In fact, people tell Melissa that when she smiles she uses her whole face! She is a child of great grace and endurance who faces her physical differences and difficulties with a positive attitude.

Today Melissa is seizure-free, stands tall, and will tell anyone she meets "I'm hearing-impaired, you know." Once, when my wife tried to arrange Melissa's hair to cover her ears so that her hearing aids wouldn't show, she told her, "Mom, that's who I am. People just have to accept me this way. I don't think it matters at all." You know, she's right.

The message to our children is that there is nothing at all they need to do to deserve or increase our love for them. On the other side of that coin, there is nothing they can do to change our love for them. But *loving* them just as they are does not mean *leaving* them just as they are.

What Love Can Do

Our love is that which enables them to cope, to deal with life, to make the transition from child to adult, from dependent to independent. It is not contingent on behavior. Love based on receiving reciprocal love quickly depletes when the person becomes "unlovely."

While serving as first lady, Pat Nixon was touring a hospital. She stopped by a bed to visit a young woman who had been blinded by rubella. After talking several minutes, she hugged the young girl and continued to talk affectionately and even sang to her. After she left the hospital she was informed that the young girl was deaf as well as blind. One of the supervisors stated, "I'm sorry, but she didn't understand a word you said."

Mrs. Nixon replied, "I knew that, but she can understand love."

The next time you have that feeling of desperation—"I can't talk to her. She doesn't hear a word I say"—you can be sure that she does understand your love, whether she shows it outwardly or not.

Love That Sets Children Free

Truly loving your children means letting them go—allowing them to explore and trusting God to finish the work you have begun. "Being confident of this very thing, that he who has begun a good work in you [and in your child] will complete it until the day of Jesus Christ" (Phil. 1:6).

The brilliant theologian and gifted preacher Thomas Aquinas was kidnapped as a young man from the Dominican Order by his own family. He was held captive at home for a year before his mother helped him to escape. Was he kidnapped because he was rebellious? No, it was because the path he was choosing seemed to his father to be a waste of a young life. His father had other plans, "better" plans, for his son.[5] But no matter how good the intention, we cannot plan and calendar our children's lives.

Some parents want to keep their children occupied at every moment—not always for the benefit of the child but for themselves. Busy is not always profitable, particularly when it comes to the impression we make on our children of their importance to our own enjoyment and sense of fulfillment.

Other parents think of time spent with their children as only a part of their overall scheme for them. Are you guilty of trying to schedule quality time as though it were a profitable business appointment? While setting aside a definite time is a worthy goal, it is only the beginning.

Not that you shouldn't enjoy or benefit from time spent with your child. In fact, the development of love and respect occurs in the small, the natural, the unique ideas you and your family enjoy. In *Parenting by Heart*, author Ron Taffel talks about "Parent Chums":

1. When you can't remember the last time you did something one on one with your child, *do something*. Even fifteen minutes makes a big difference.

2. When you can't remember the last time *you* enjoyed yourself *with* your child, do something *you* like to do and take your child along.[6]

To quote Mother Teresa again: "Love begins at home. It is not how much we do, but how much love we put in the action that we do."

The Search for Significance

Dr. Robert McGee is president of the Rapha treatment centers and author of the excellent book, *The Search for Significance*. According to Dr. McGee, most psychiatrists agree that a lack of self-esteem can cause kids to follow the crowd blindly or to give in to temptation. Opinions vary, however, on how to build that self-esteem. But McGee believes the key component of building self-esteem in kids is helping them achieve *a sense of personal significance*. He points out that most teens consider that what they do—their success in sports, grades, friends, and so on—is the measure of who they are. As a result, very few learn to deal with disappointment, with failure, and even fewer are willing to get up and try again.

An estimated 8 million Americans, the majority of them women, are imprisoned by the eating disorder anorexia. Of course this is, in one sense, a symptom of a larger problem. "The most widespread disease in the world is an inferiority complex," states author Sterling Sill. When you look at the way clothing fads float in and out of our lives, you can better understand that, for the teen, trying on a new style may signify "trying on" a new personality. Be patient. Don't make a big deal about clothing unless it's immodest or totally inappropriate in some way. For example, dressing in all black on occasion is all right as an experiment, but if it becomes a way of life it could be a signal of a developing problem.

All my life I was told I was a nobody who would never amount to anything. But I have read that everybody is a "Thumbody." Because no two thumbprints are the same, no two people are the same. As Ethel Waters used to say before she sang at the Billy Graham crusades, "I know I'm a somebody because God don't make no junk!"

The Big Search

In the youth edition of *Search for Significance*, authors McGee and McCallister call this longing for identity and caring the "big search." There seems to be a deep longing or craving inside most people for something more. This is the case in the one who pretends to be like someone else because he doesn't like himself, the person who uses drugs and alcohol to please his friends, or the young lady who is sexually active to fill the craving for love and affection. This universal search was described in the hit country-western song, "Looking for Love in All the Wrong Places."

McGee and McCallister warn of several traps into which young people are easily ensnared:

1. The Performance Trap—"I must meet certain standards to feel good about myself."
2. The Approval Trap—"I must be approved or accepted by certain people to accept myself."
3. The Blame Game Trap—"If I fail I am unworthy of love and deserve to be blamed and condemned."
4. The Shame Trap—"I am what I am. I cannot change. I am hopeless."[7]

"The greatest way to build self-esteem is through praise and encouragement," declares Zig Ziglar, motivational speaker and author of *Raising Positive Kids in a Negative World*. Kids need someone to believe in them, someone who will say, "Yes, you can do it. Yes, you are a special someone." Their greatest need is for someone who loves them day in and day out regardless of behavior or accomplishment.

One psychologist told me that her office is filled with teens who say, "I know they [their parents] love me, but it just seems so empty, so fake." What she is really saying is that there is no intimacy. Whether time together is structured or grabbed, there should always be an impression of one another, a glimpse into one another's personality, an enjoyment of togetherness upon which memories and a continued relationship can build.

It is difficult to ascertain which comes first: Does poor self-esteem lead to an inability for intimacy, or does the lack of intimacy lead to poor self-esteem? The child who cannot relate intimately with peers is a child crying out for help. Her loneliness feels to her like a black hole, so anyone or anything that offers to pull her out of the hole and show her warmth will be accepted. Anyone, that is, but the family who doesn't seem to understand.

Help your child to identify his style and then encourage him to pursue it. There must be *something* he can excel at. It is an absolute imperative that he find it. No one can go through life *feeling* like a failure without finally *becoming* a failure.

For centuries, various cultures had rituals for "coming of age," marking a child's passage into adulthood. The Jewish ceremony of bar mitzvah for boys and bat mitzvah for girls at the age of thirteen is one in which the child is declared to be a young adult. In some countries, Jewish parents make a verbal contract with the child with the promise of increased freedom, and the child responds with the agreement to increased responsibilities.

Of course the age of maturity—in physical, emotional, social, and spiritual areas—differs for each child. We cannot dictate one specific ceremony at one specific time. There may be a great value, however, in the idea of a ceremony in which parents acknowledge that the child is growing into adulthood and the child acknowledges the decision to accept the responsibility of independence.

Such a ceremony should be creatively designed, should reflect the child's individual personality, and have a definite air of celebration. Commitments to each other and certain rules could be discussed together. Passages of Scripture could be selected and written down in a book of agreement. No gifts other than the gift of time and love should be brought to this ceremony.

I stress writing down the agreements and commitments because of the almost omnipresent threat of misunderstanding. Having something in writing could prevent situations in which the child says, "I wasn't sure how you'd feel about it. That's not what I thought you meant. It didn't seem like it would be a problem or a big deal." Over and over the parent and child can refer to the book of agreement, amending and changing it when necessary. Signatures should be used each time, as well as dates.

This also works for day-to-day responsibilities. A contract is drawn up detailing daily and weekly chores, dating rules, television, allowances, etc. Each one can look at his or her contract and find no surprises.

Expressing Personal Faith

The pronouncement that a child is a young adult should carry with it the understanding of the need to search out feelings and beliefs. Dr. Paul Tournier, in his book *The Whole Person in a Broken World*, describes this as the removal of the "coat" of the parents' morality and the "knitting" of the individual's own coat.[8] He goes on to say that it is normal and even necessary for this to be a time of some crisis.

In my crusades, I see hundreds of teens who come forward to make a personal commitment to the Lord. Their parents are often shocked and say, "But he/she already did that years ago." What they don't seem to understand is the teen's intense need to make this a personal, "grown-up" decision of the heart. It is a time which says that faith is no longer only the result of the teaching and belief of the parents, but an expression of the child's own conviction and faith. Whether or not this is a salvation experience is not the question. The youth now lays down the guilty burden of thoughts or actions of the past and resolves to walk in the path of the will of God.

Children must be taught more than right and wrong. They must understand that they are under *God's* authority, not just their parents'. It must be clear in their mind that these are the laws of the Holy God who loves them and not just some things mom and dad decided to rule their life with.

The goal is to bring them to the decision to stand for Christ on their own. Does this have to mean isolation? No! It is a time of special need for parental leadership and example. We can pray that our children will grow in faith and fortitude, that they will make a difference, being voices and not echoes in our world.

Accepting Responsibility

Another rite of passage is learning to accept responsibility, especially for wrongdoing. Learning to say "I'm sorry" is a requirement for becoming a responsible adult.

Taking responsibility for mistakes doesn't always have to be made publicly. In our family altar time, we use journals. Everyone has a notebook with plain, loose-leaf paper. It is sectioned off for prayer requests, Bible study notes, and for writing letters to the Lord. I encourage my teens to write down their thoughts and share them with the rest of us only if they want to.

The paramount goal of parents is to lead their children to transfer the love and respect they have for their parents to love and respect for the living Lord. As small children they will obey out of love for us; as young adults they will obey out of love for God.

Remember that the powerful Word of God never returns void. Again, you are not looking for immediate results. You are seeking to lay a foundation for growing into a responsible, caring, person who is able to resolve conflict and endure disappointment.

13

Get Out the Big Guns

The Patriot Missile of Prayer

During the Persian Gulf War, the Allies were desperate for high-tech weaponry that would make our victory sure. While it appeared that the Patriot missile was the new kid on the block, it had actually been twenty-five years in the making. The missile system was produced through a combination of old-fashioned American knowhow and the experience of what worked and didn't work in past wars. In spite of its accuracy, no chances were taken. For every Iraqi Scud missile launched, our defense sent up two Patriots to meet it.[1]

Similarly, parents are desperate for the latest statistic, gimmick, technique, or information that will enable them to win the battle for the minds and hearts of their kids. We buy parenting books. We read them, make notes, and highlight passages. We attend seminars, listen intently, and make goals and lists. Then we try to implement what we've learned, putting every ounce of our emotion and love into our children.

All this is good and sometimes can produce visible and immediate results. They are actions over which we have some control. Yet in ministering to our children we must remember the assessment Paul made of his ability to minister: "Not that we are sufficient of ourselves to think of anything as being from ourselves, but our sufficiency is from God" (2 Cor. 3:5).

Just because we seem to be in charge of our families doesn't mean we are in charge of our children's growth and stability. In any realistic assessment of the hope we have to raise godly children, there is one element more important than all the rest. It is more important than our hard work and diligence, vital though those are. It carries more weight than our knowledge and insight, as necessary as those are. The one thing without which all of our parenting is little more than a shot in the dark is . . . prayer.

We all say we believe in prayer, yet it often receives the least of our energy. Christian parents need to keep ever before them that the "unforgivable sin" (if we can be so bold) in the realm of parenting is the failure to pray for their children.

The Battle We Face

If we are truly to grasp the urgency of a committed prayer life for our children we must begin to think in terms of a spiritual world and a spiritual battle. Jesus Himself taught us to pray for deliverance from evil influence: "Do not lead us into temptation, but deliver us from the evil one" (Matt. 6:13). His prayer for us in John 17:15 is significant in seeing the needs of our children: "I do not pray that You should take them out of the world, but that You should keep them from the evil one." The Lord was speaking of the spiritual world where we walk and war daily.

In Luke 22:31–32, Jesus told Peter, "Satan has asked for you . . . but I have prayed for you." In Job 1:6–12, the account is given of Satan coming before the throne and asking personally for permission to buffet Job.

While we argue and cry over every petty thing, we are losing the battle for our children—mainly because we are fighting the wrong enemy. It is not the child we must fight, but the roaring lion who seeks to devour him. "For we do not wrestle against flesh and blood, but against principalities, against powers, against the rulers of the darkness of this age, against spiritual hosts of wickedness in the heavenly places" (Eph. 6:12).

The Weapon of Prayer

To fight a spiritual foe, we need a spiritual weapon—the weapon of prayer. Elisha prayed and a boy was raised to life. Jesus prayed and Lazarus was raised from the dead. We must first get power from God in prayer if we are to see our weak or spiritually dead children raised to health (Eph. 2:1).

Traveling and speaking across the country and around the world in middle and senior high schools, my heart is broken by the hardness of hearts, the blatant disregard for what is good, and the "feel good" attitude that rules the lives of teens. But then, through the crowd, I spot the few—the strong Christian young people who stand tall and go against the flow. They look different. They walk different. They wear genuine smiles. These young people intrigue me, and I always try to get to know them and their families in the hope that I will discover some "magic" formula or new idea.

'On My Knees'

Two of our dearest friends, Claude and Janice Thomas of Euless, Texas, have raised four morally and spiritually strong, God-fearing, motivated, confident young men. Two have followed a call to the ministry, one is an attorney, and the other is a godly influence and leader in his high school. This family has so inspired me that I sat the parents down and took notebook and pen in hand, ready to capture their "recipe" for successful parenting and children of faith. "What did you do? How did you do it?" I asked.

Claude looked at me and said, "By faith."

Janice smiled and replied, "On my knees." She explained that every morning at 5:30 she would rise to pray for her children. As a young mother she had read Lamentations 2:19 and felt this verse come alive in her heart: "Arise, cry out in the night, at the beginning of the watches; pour out your heart like water before the face of the Lord. Lift your hands toward Him for the life of your young children."

Of all the advice I've ever heard or read, those three words have had more impact on me than any volume—"On my knees." Often in my mind I see a portrait of that dear mother on her knees crying out for her children before God, pleading for their protection from the evil one. There has never been a nobler warrior.

For our children the burden of approaching adulthood seems greater than they can bear. At this time when independence seems to grow, the need to pray increases dramatically.

Paul's Prayer, My Prayer

In asking God to show me how to pray and what to pray for my children, I found myself one day reading Colossians 1:9–11. I certainly do not claim this is the best way or the only way to pray, but I do want to share with you my personal prayers for my loved ones through these verses. The apostle Paul wrote:

> For this reason we also, since the day we heard it, do not cease to pray for you, and to ask that you may be filled with the knowledge of His will in all wisdom and spiritual understanding; that you may walk worthy of the Lord, fully pleasing Him, being fruitful in every good work and increasing in the knowledge of God; strengthened with all might, according to His glorious power, for all patience and longsuffering with joy.
>
> Colossians 1:9–11

"We do not cease to pray." This is speaking of earnest prayer offered constantly to God in a way that increases in intensity as our children grow older; for as they are growing they need prayers that will grow with them.

"That you may be filled." We want our children to experience nothing less than the abundant life that Jesus promised in John 10:10: "I have come that they might have life, and that they may have it more abundantly."

Kids seem to thrive on looking for fun, and they complain more and more of boredom. Pray that they will enjoy life and learn the value of simple pleasures without being addicted to wastefulness (which is the definition of "prodigal"). Pray also that we can teach them to make good use of their discretionary time.

"With the knowledge of His will." To be headed in the right direction, every person must know the individual plan and purpose of God for his life. Pray that each child will seek God's best

for her future, and that the experiences of these years will act to prosper that future through the establishment of good habits.

I also pray daily that God will place people into my children's lives who will influence them for good. I have asked Him to send godly friends and acquaintances as well as worthy heroes into their path as one more step in following the will of God.

"In all wisdom." This wisdom (Gk. *sophia*) is the knowledge of first principles, the foundation of mental excellence. Pray daily for your kids to have the ability to learn well in school and in life. Pray for them to have good study skills and habits, good memory retention, and an excellent relationship with their teachers.[2]

"Spiritual understanding." In order to apply the first principles, the basic knowledge, they need daily spiritual intelligence and insight. Here, parents should also pray for their children to begin to develop spiritual independence, to transfer from mom and dad's faith to their own. Though this takes place over a period of time, it might also involve a rite-of-passage experience, as we discussed earlier.

Pray that they will begin to trust God to meet their needs and to answer their prayers. One way to do this is to encourage them in the use of a prayer journal with a place to check off prayers that have been answered.

Pray that the truth and teachings of the Scriptures given to them as children will move from their heads to their hearts. Scripture memorization, also, is extremely valuable because of the promise that the Word of God will not return void, but it will accomplish that which God pleases.

"That you may walk worthy." Here it is again—"good" kids. The walk described here is one of total conduct in the course of life. It is not a "be good today" but a decision of the heart to walk in the convictions already presented as the will of God, that they might fully understand what is right and wrong. Here we pray for responsibility, morality, and the overcoming of temptation.

Jesus prayed for His followers in John 17:17, "Sanctify them by Your truth. Your word is truth." Pray that your children will be set apart for the special task of leadership through a godly testimony, that they will be an influence, instead of being influenced.

Jesus further prayed, "I do not pray that You should take them out of the world, but that You should keep them from the evil one" (v. 15).

"Fully pleasing Him." I want so much for my children to find a place of service for the Lord. Not only is this the task of every Christian, but it is a great lesson for their spirit of honor answering honor. Both of my girls teach and work in a preschool Sunday school class and love it. I couldn't keep them away if I tried, because they receive even more than they give.

Finding a place of meaningful service also gives an opportunity to grow into a love for the church. I pray that my children will be committed to turning to the church both when they need a blessing and when they want to be a blessing.

When children learn to serve God, they learn to relate rightly to other people. They learn humility and the principle of give-love-to-receive-love firsthand.

"Being fruitful in every good work." Every parent wants a successful life for his or her child. The pride of achievement through responsibility and hard work is an energizing force. Pray for good grades on tests, the ability to make the cut for the team, courage during an audition, and so on. Few kids can win at everything they are doing, but they can learn a winning spirit in all that they do. This is the description of a fruitful life, that every experience builds them into the persons God would have them be.

Then, if they do poorly on that test, or fail to make the cut, pray that you can still be supportive and affirming. Many kids never learn to deal with discouragement, and this lack often carries over into their adult life. A child whose self-esteem is smashed over failure will be an adult whose self-esteem is easily destroyed. Pray that each endeavor, win or lose, will be fruitful and thus strengthen character.

"Increasing in the knowledge of God." When I think of the thousands of college students I speak to who refuse to go to church now that they are away from the rule of their parents, I know in my heart that they have never understood the majesty of who God is.

My youngest daughter is studying an evangelism course for teens, and she told me the two ways that the average child or teen thinks of God: (1) He's a grandfather who will never punish anybody because He loves them too much—and the other grandchildren are worse, anyway; and (2) He's a policeman who writes everything down, and if He catches you, you'll be under His angry control.

Pray for children to discover the majesty and wonder of who God is. In one family time we were making acrostics for the names of God. When we got to the "I" in Elohim, Melissa suggested "interesting." Teach your children the fullness of God's character, the deep reality of His love, and the security of His holiness.

"Strengthened with all might." I was praying in earnest one day for God to protect my girls from evil when suddenly I had a strong conviction to amend my prayer. In addition to protection, I felt compelled to pray for them to have strength to stand up as a leader. We need to remember that being strong enough to say no is only the start. I pray earnestly for my girls to have the insight to know when and why to say no.

I pray for strength in the spiritual warfare and also that they will learn to use and remember to use each weapon given in Ephesians 6. I pray that they will remember the escape promised in 1 Corinthians 10:13, and that they will first consider fighting the enemy.

You cannot always be present to encourage your children personally as they battle temptations daily, but you can be present in spirit by praying through Ephesians 6:13–17 with them in mind:

> Take up the whole armor of God, that you may be able to withstand in the evil day. . . . Stand therefore, having girded your waist with truth, having put on the breastplate of righteousness, and having shod your feet with the preparation of the gospel of peace; above all, taking the shield of faith with which you will be able to quench all the fiery darts of the wicked one. And take the helmet of salvation, and the sword of the Spirit, which is the word of God.

"For all patience." This seems a contradiction in terms for any child or teen who "can't wait to grow up." Before each birthday gets to the halfway mark, we are reminded of the next. Every

"How old are you?" is answered with "almost . . . ," even if the birthday is months away!

The kind of patience Paul is praying for here is patience with people, the ability to get along with difficult folks who might try to crush a child's spirit and weaken her pride of conviction. Pray daily that they can deal with the unlovely without becoming irritated, without bitterness, and without retaliation. For a child, this need for patience might be especially felt in a teacher-student relationship where the child feels unfairly singled out or judged.

"Longsuffering with joy." Pray for fortitude to conquer and deal triumphantly with life. In the Greek language, this is a picture of turning "burdens into glory." In the nineties we say "Make lemons into lemonade." Pray for self-restraint and even-temperedness on a consistent basis. Not only are we praying for this endurance, but that it will be an endurance of joy. We know that all joy is built on faith in Christ which is enduring, and not on circumstances which are fleeting.

It is up to us to believe that this indeed is our greatest work as parents—to be prayer warriors on behalf of our children. We should not only pray *about* them, but *for* them.

We should stay away from "prayer pockets"—saying the same prayer over and over for the one character flaw or the one change we believe needs to be made. Pray for the whole child, for every area of life. As the whole healing and strengthening takes place, that particular pocket you are worried about will take care of itself.

Our praying cannot be a weak offering or a passing journal note, but a passionate, disciplined act of the heart.

Standing in the Gap

In the Book of Ezekiel, God came to the prophet saying, "I looked for a man to stand in the gap." The loving parent says, "Here am I, Lord. I will stand in the gap for my child." With one hand raised to heaven, holding on to the heart and hand of God, we reach out with the other to clasp the heart and hand of our child.

We stand in the gap for the one who cannot or will not pray, for the one who needs our ever-present prayer support. Urgently, earnestly, as we have never prayed before, we pray. Urgently, earnestly, He promises, "I will listen."

Whatever else you do, pray for your kids!

14

Tearing Down the Chemical Curtain

How to Keep Your Kids from Ever Using Drugs

It can start out quite innocently. Your child is at a friend's house for a party. Every one of his friends seems to be there, including that special someone. The music is really cooking in the background. There is laughter and good times for all.

Suddenly, like a bolt of lightning, with no warning, a friend hands your child a can of beer or a wine cooler. There it is, one of those pressure-cooker moments that can determine your teenager's life.

Parents and church suddenly seem far, far away. Everyone at the party seems to be looking at him. Your child thinks, *Well, man, everybody here is drinking. All of my friends are drinking. They're just having fun. What's the harm in a beer anyway? What's the big deal?*

If we as parents have not prepared our children for that moment and other crisis moments beforehand, we may have already made their decision for them. Put yourself in their shoes for just one day. If you can do that, I believe you will better understand the tremendous pressures they face to conform and to belong.

Our Alcoholic Atmosphere

A young person sits down to watch a favorite show when a commercial explodes across the scene promising, "It just doesn't get any better than this!" "This" is the scene of the beautiful people playing on the beach and relaxing with a cold one. The girls are wearing what I call "dental floss" bathing suits. The sun is setting, a yacht is anchored in the background, and a beautiful young woman is shown in an intimate moment with her male friend and two wine coolers. As a young person sees the glittery commercial and compares it to his normal life, he feels like he's been left out of life's party. Alcohol, portrayed as the "cure for what ails you" makes a big impression as the possible missing link.

The advertisements are not the only problem with television today. Television drama is at least as bad, perhaps worse. Dramas make every claim to show life "as it is," and today's television programs portray drinking as a fact of life. The reward for a "hard day's night" is "you deserve a drink." From the famous athlete to the hip comedian, everyone seems to be saying, "Drinking will drown your problems."

Ironically your child doesn't need to watch television to receive the message that alcohol is not only acceptable but essential. Millions of parents consume alcohol on a daily basis. In fact, alcohol is consumed in 70 percent of our nation's homes. As a young man growing up, I received the standard lectures about not drinking. Those words of advice were not very effective in my case, however. Why not? Well, simply because there was a six-pack in the refrigerator, a row of bottles in the liquor cabinet, and an array of pills in the medicine cabinet.

Alcohol Is a Drug

My first book was entitled *Drugs and Drinking: What Every Parent and Teen Should Know*. The common fallacy that liquor is "not as bad as marijuana or cocaine" is far from the truth. Alcohol is the greatest drug problem our nation faces. Consider these facts:

- Alcohol is a "gateway drug." Ninety-eight out of every hundred addicts who seek medical help or treatment for marijuana, PCP, crack, cocaine, or heroin use have confessed they began with alcohol.

- Alcohol is the number one killer of young people between the ages of fifteen and twenty-four.

- Three-fourths of adult problem drinkers and adult alcoholics started drinking as teenagers.

- Alcohol is the leading cause of divorce, spouse abuse, child abuse, traffic fatalities, incest, and suicide.

- Every seven minutes an American child is arrested for a drug offense: 76,986 a year. Whether consumed alone or used with other drugs, alcohol contributes to suicide and to homicide, the second and third leading causes of death among our nation's youth.

- Every thirty minutes an American child is arrested for drunk driving: 17,674 a year.

- Alcohol use is beginning at a frighteningly younger age, often between the ages of ten and thirteen. Quite simply, it is too accessible. It may begin with a parent giving a child a beer. Remember, one can of beer contains the same level of alcohol as a one-and-a-half-ounce shot of straight whiskey.[1]

Some three years ago I spoke at a large metropolitan high school in Houston. A young man named Rodney, a senior, asked me if I would walk him to his locker. As we joked we made our way to his locker. It was obvious that he was troubled and wanted to talk. He had just sat through forty-five minutes of our high school assembly program entitled "Straight Talk," where I had shared about my own youthful struggles with alcohol and drugs. When we got to his locker he showed me a thermos. It was full of gin. He said, "Jay, I've never admitted this to anyone, but since you talked about being a teenage alcoholic, I believe I can talk to you. I've been drinking since I was eleven."

I found out that his father had left when Rodney was ten, running off with his mom's sister, and I learned what that abandonment had done to their family. He talked about how bitter and angry he was. When he drank, he said, his problems seemed to fade away. He started drinking at all the school functions—

every dance, every ball game, every date. Soon he became a
teenage alcoholic. He said to me that day, "Jay, you quit. I want
to quit, too."

Widespread Availability

The one thing that parents fail to understand is that both
alcohol and drugs are easily accessible to teens. It is available everywhere—in a best friend's home, sometimes in the homes of
church members. So many parents are working, so many children
are home hours upon hours by themselves with alcohol just sitting
there.

Even if alcohol were not available in our homes, "smart"
teens can get it by simply asking a willing adult if he would like
to make a buck or two and buy it for them. There is also the occasional unscrupulous store owner who will sell to teens at a
marked-up price.

Alcohol and drug abuse pose one of the largest health, legal,
and social dangers in America today. Millions of our nation's
youth are trapped behind the chemical curtain of drug abuse and
drowning in a sea of alcohol. America's reliance on drugs is un-
equalled in the history of mankind. Sixty-five percent of the
world's illicit drugs are consumed by Americans.

Even more devastating is the National Institute on Drug
Abuse's (NIDA) latest statistics which reveal that America's
teenagers continue to "show the highest level of drug use of
young people anywhere in the world." The NIDA also declares
that the marijuana that is available on our streets today is far
more potent than any that had been available before. It is believed that, due to the availability, the affordability, and the
potency of cocaine, and especially crack cocaine, the marijuana
growers have been forced to greatly increase the THC level in
marijuana. THC is the primary psychoactive agent that determines the potency or the effect of marijuana. This means that
even occasional or moderate use of marijuana is threatening to
one's health. The American Medical Association has an-
nounced, "Without question marijuana use affects and impairs

the learning, the memory, and the general intellectual development of a young person's brain. It can also disrupt and harm the
reproductive organs, especially in developing youth."

You Can Run but You Can't Hide

Parents who are deeply concerned have often thought of
moving to rural America to protect their children. They feel that
if they leave the city and move to the country or smaller towns,
their children will have a better environment. But a recent General Accounting Office (GAO) report indicates that alcohol and
drug abuse is as serious in rural America as it is in the urban areas.

There are some differences, however. Rural states have a
higher arrest rate for illegal use of alcohol than for illegal drugs.
Marijuana, inhalants, and stimulants pose more rural problems
than does cocaine. But there is also the problem of fewer treatment centers in rural ares. The GAO report acknowledges that
many rural treatment centers have found it difficult to attract and
keep staffers, and they have found that it is too expensive to hire
the needed drug specialists.[2]

Teenage Drug Use

In spite of the war on drug abuse, there has been a marked
increase of trauma centers having to deal with drug overdoses
and related problems. Emergency room situations involving
drugs increased almost sixfold in a recent four-year period, from
8,831 incidents in 1984 to 46,820 in 1988. Cocaine-related
deaths increased from 628 to 1,589 in the same period. Crack
remains the drug of choice among inner-city youth, and it shows
no sign of abatement.[3]

Rodney's descent into alcoholism followed a fairly typical
pattern. A very similar pattern applies to dependency on other
drugs. Knowing these stages might be an early warning system to
help you keep your children from getting hooked. Just as there are
typical stages of alcoholism among young people, there are also
distinct levels of abuse in the case of other drugs.

Stage 1: Exposure and Experimentation

First there is the stage at which a child or teen (and remember the age is getting younger and younger) is exposed to drugs. It usually begins with experimentation. Unfortunately, this occurs far too often at home, when the child sneaks a beer from the refrigerator, or an older brother or sister invites the younger sibling to partake. Even worse, this recreational use can sometimes involve the parents.

In my book, *Drugs and Drinking*, I noted that junior-high-age students, especially boys, are great experimenters with various types of mood-altering substances. Some may never go beyond the experimental stage. They decide that chemical use is not for them. But many who try once will continue to try and some will even become regular users. Some even will begin to use beer and pot in this stage and will learn to seek and enjoy the mood swings that these substances provide.

Stage 2: Actively Seeking Drugs

The second stage is the progression (or *digression*) stage when the child actively seeks out the drug. At first it may be just a fad, or bowing to peer pressure. "You know I'm no chicken." "Hey, I can do anything you can do." Then it becomes a habit or a psychological dependence. In the progression stage you feel in your mind that you *need* this drug. "It makes me feel better." "I can handle stress better." "I'm funnier." "I'm hipper." "I'm wittier." It is during this stage that changes in behavior start.

Several changes in the drug user can occur at this stage. Often moral, social, family, and religious values begin to deteriorate. There will also be physical changes, including the neglect of personal hygiene and appearance, especially when under the influence. The user will demonstrate a restless, bored attitude that is exhibited, not only in dress, but in language and in the choice of friends.

The user's personality will begin to change, which may be reflected in areas such as grades, school attendance, and involvement in sports. Emotional flareups, outbreaks of temper, and withdrawal from the family will occur. The young drug abuser may need more money, and parents may notice that money around the house begins to disappear. Overall, *change* is the major symptom of drug abuse.

A child who exhibits abuse at this early age may be establishing a lifelong pattern. The chemical use may level off and stay at the "social/recreational" level, causing no interpersonal conflict or externally harmful consequences, or it may move quickly to a more advanced level of dependency.

It is difficult to assess chemical dependency at this stage because drug use is often limited to weekends. The normal turmoil of adolescence is baffling enough to both teenagers and their parents; we must be cautious about evaluating how deep the problem runs. Many students have been inappropriately labeled as "dependent" when they aren't—yet. They may be using drugs occasionally on the weekend, but that alone does not make them dependent. I refer to those who use drugs recreationally as "weekend warriors." They may still be going to church on Sunday and may be working a weekend job at a fast-food place, yet they will use drugs in social circumstances or social settings.

This is sometimes referred to as the "regular use" stage. Simply using more does not by itself indicate dependency, but a pattern of regular use coupled with some adverse behavioral changes can show a definite move toward possible dependency. The point here is not *how much* is being used or *how often*, but *why* it is being used and what behavioral changes occur as the result of the use.

If teenagers have to lie to their parents about their savings account, about why they've dropped out of school sports and other activities, and about who their companions are, and if they have to maintain these fictions in order to continue to use drugs, they often begin to experience guilt. Unfortunately, this guilt produces feelings of self-hate, which results in increased drug use. A cycle begins, consisting of use/guilt/remorse/increased use.

Stage 3: Preoccupation with Drugs

Preoccupation with drugs is one of the major indicators of a chemical problem. More and more of the student's time, energy, and money are spent thinking about being high and ensuring that a steady supply of drugs is available. Questioning a user at this stage will reveal that very few of his or her daily activities do not include drug use. The user accepts this as normal.

Periodic problems with parents and police may serve to cause the abuser to decide that it would be smart to cut down or quit using all together. He may succeed for several weeks. Generally, these periods of abstinence will not last. They do serve, however, to strengthen the abuser's sincere delusion that there is no problem, that he can quit at any time. But even though the abuser thinks he can still make a choice, he often forgets the fact that the choice he makes is always the same—to keep using.

Stage 4: Real Dependence

By the time users reach this stage, negative personal feelings and psychological and physical dependence have been building steadily to the point that they require daily, even hourly medication with drugs. Abusers in this state are unable to distinguish between normal and intoxicated behavior. For them, being high is normal and no rational or moral argument can break through their chemically maintained delusion.

This delusion persists even in the face of overwhelming evidence that their abuse is out of control and is physically, mentally, and emotionally strangling them. These abusers will continue to insist that there is no problem, that they are not out of control, and that they can quit at any time. Obviously, at this stage they need immediate treatment.

Drugproofing Your Home

Parents must realize that the home is the place where the greatest influence can be exerted upon their children. Don't let anyone try to convince you that you really have no control or influence over your child. The fact is, healthy homes can become a fortress of prevention against many problems, including drug abuse.

The Power of Love

Parents, the first step that you can take to keep your kids from ever using drugs is to make a commitment to love each other. When mom and dad love each other and are committed to each other, they provide an environment of growth. Parents can build their child's self-image and self-esteem through love and respect for each other. The more that you are willing to work on your relationship as a couple, the better prepared you will be for the challenges of parenting.

When things are going wrong in a marriage they tend to influence and distort everything else in the family. Kids need to be reassured that their world is not going to fall apart because mom and dad are going to split up. The security of a loving and stable family is vital to your child's own stability, success, and maturity. The more you as a couple are willing to invest in each other, the more you are ultimately investing in the future of your children.

Of course this love must spill over onto the children, too. When my children were much younger, we use to play a game called "The Psychologist Says." I began to tell my young daughters that if I did not hug and kiss them a lot, when they grew up to be teenagers they would run wild. Therefore, for their own good, I would have to tickle them and to kiss them. Obviously, as we played this game my girls would squeal and run and hide.

One day I came upon my youngest daughter, Christina, with our basset hound, Pharaoh, pinned to the floor, telling him that if she did not hug him and kiss him that he would run with the bad dogs in the neighborhood. Without question, the first line of defense is to love each other.

Plan for the Storms

The second thing that parents can do is to anticipate storms in family life, in their marriage, and in the economy. Remember that there will be bumpy roads along the way of your child's development to adulthood. Change brings stress. Anticipate that your child will be undergoing tremendous changes. Tastes and dislikes, favorite colors, hobbies, and emotions will vary as they grow older. Taking change in stride and not allowing every storm to throw the home off course will communicate stability to your children.

Accentuate the Positive

Third, parents must learn to emphasize the positive. Find out what your children are doing right and praise them. For example, when you hear someone handling a difficult situation over the phone, diffusing a point of contention, compliment her right then—on the spot. Too often we instruct our children only about what they have done wrong. "I'd better not ever catch you doing that again." "You'd better not ever say that again." "I don't like what you've been doing." Break the cycle of negative behavior by bragging on your child when you find him doing something right.

I believe the greatest priority of parents, especially those who have a living faith, is to put a sweet taste in the mouth of their children for the things of God. I've seen parents who refused to have alcohol or tobacco or any drugs in their home, and yet they are often caustic and critical by nature. We need to help our children see that a life lived for God will be a positive and wonderful experience. It's life changing. It's exciting! It's fulfilling!

I like the picture painted by historians who describe how Hebrew midwives would help newborn babies enter the world. After assisting in the delivery, the midwife would cut the umbilical cord, clean the baby up, and prepare a sweet-tasting pabulum. It would be a kind of paste made of pomegranates, coconut milk, honey, and sugar. The midwife would put a bit of it in the mouth of that child and the child would love the sweetness and would pucker up and hunger for more. My goal in the life of my daughters is to put a sweet taste in their mouths for what life is all about, and especially the abundant life of living for the Lord.

Help Children Develop a Skill

Dr. James Dobson stated it well when he said on a radio broadcast that the failure to help a son or daughter to learn one skill that they will be good at, one thing that will help increase their confidence level and strengthen their self-image, is like sending them naked into their adolescent years. I agree. If we do not equip our children with at least one thing, one thing that they can look to for self-confidence and self-esteem—whether it be sports, crafts, drama, etc.—then we've left them at the mercy of the crowd because the crowd will make them find something they are good at.

I remember a high school friend who was nicknamed "The Sponge." Why? Because he could drink more alcohol than anyone we knew. I had another buddy who was a better fist-fighter than anyone else—the toughest guy in our school. As for me, I was always the class clown. I could always be counted on to take a dare, to do something funny. When I think about it now, I can hardly believe some of the foolish and dangerous risks that I took in order for a few people to accept me (which is really no acceptance at all).

What kind of badge of honor does your son or daughter wear? Are they accepted by the crowd because they are good at getting high, or because they have a reputation for being a sexual star? As parents, let us endeavor to help them find the one skill that will equip them for the tough times of adolescence.

Teach Them to Stand Alone

The next step in drugproofing your children is to teach them to have the courage to take a stand for what they believe, and, if necessary, to stand alone. We need to recognize that most teenagers would prefer to be in the wrong and be with their friends than to do what is right and be alone. Studies have revealed that teenagers have almost a deadly fear—a paranoia—of not being accepted.

You will notice that children vary in their attitudes about this. My oldest daughter, Melissa, has the attitude that if you don't like her there is something wrong with you. My youngest daughter, Christina, however, who is equally loved and equally gifted, tends to be very susceptible to what the crowd thinks. When you evaluate your children, take their individual differences into consideration.

When I talk to Melissa and Christa about their need to be able to stand alone and to resist the tug of the crowd, I don't say it in a tone of condemnation. I say, "Honey, you do all these things right, but the one area we need to work on—and frankly it was an area I was very weak in—is that you must learn to stand alone. Don't just go along with the crowd."

I try to picture this for them by using an analogy. Before I get on an airplane I check several times to be sure that the plane is going to the destination where I need to go. Our children need to be sure they're with the people who can take them to the right destination.

Teach your children the "arrive alive" mentality. Although I've found that scare tactics are not usually effective with young people, true-life stores (an article in the paper or something on the news) concerning a tragic death of a teenager, an overdose, or someone killed while driving while drunk affords a tremendous opportunity to teach at a time when the child may be truly listening.

As parents we understand that teenagers have a desperate need to belong to a group. Some of these groups can strengthen them, and some can cause them to deteriorate or even destroy them.

Clean Up Your Own Act!

One very practical step toward drugproofing your children is to clean out the medicine cabinet and throw away any prescription drugs not currently being used. One of the most popular games in middle schools and high schools across the country is called "rainbowing" or "fruit salad." Teenagers take pills from medicine cabinets at home, take them to school, and then mix them all together. Young people will randomly pick out three or four pills and take them. Prescription drugs are being greatly abused by young people.

I would not have alcohol or tobacco in my home. Tobacco is a cause for alarm partly because it prepares the lungs for marijuana and for the very harsh fumes from crack cocaine. Using tobacco can toughen the lungs and make these dangerous drugs more palatable.

Offer Something Better

Finally, *I would not prohibit without providing.* By that I mean don't forbid without providing a substitute or an alternative. Our children need us to say yes more than they need us to say no.

For the last ten years, I have been privileged to serve on various local and state drug task forces, as well as working at the national level through the executive office of the president. I worked first with Nancy Reagan's "Just Say No" effort, then closely with former Drug Czar William Bennett. Through the Office of National Drug Control Policy, I assisted in establishing a national interfaith coalition against drugs under the leadership of former Florida Governor Robert Martinez. Having now looked at the problem from many aspects, I am amazed at the complexity of this epidemic.

On the other hand, I am tremendously encouraged by the courageous efforts of so many law-enforcement personnel, teachers, counselors, administrators, ministers, and, yes, parents. Especially parents. As a parent, you can still make the greatest difference. You can be your children's fire wall of protection against the raging firestorm of drugs in our culture.

15

Departed for a Season

Living with (and without) a Prodigal

Other than death, nothing is so painful as the rejection a parent feels when a child departs from the family during a time of anger or rebellion. To a devout family, the departure of the child into a "far country, and there wasted his possessions with prodigal living" such as alcohol, drugs, and promiscuity, stings as harshly as the lash of a cat-o'-nine-tails.

An examination of Luke 15 provides insight into the "prodigal." The word means "addicted to wastefulness." It can't help but hurt a parent to see a child waste his life.

Division and disappointment seem to be part and parcel of the legacy of many families. A family may consist of two children, well adjusted and succeeding, and a third who's out of step. As a parent, you must not subject yourself to an autopsy in attempting to answer the question why or you will find that you have bled to death at your own hands.

A Prodigal Who Returned

The wonder of Scripture is that while it confronts, corrects, and challenges us as parents to shepherd our children, it provides great comfort at the same time. An example is found in the small New Testament book of Philemon. It is the story of Onesimus, a prodigal who returned. If you mourn the departure of a prodigal, use this study as a life-saving rope to pull you up from the heaviness of guilt and the anguish of what might have been.

A Slave Named "Profitable"

Philemon, to whom Paul addresses this letter, and his wife Apphia lived in the town of Colossae. Apparently he was a wealthy businessman who became a born-again Christian and allowed the newly formed church to meet in his home (Philemon 2).

The environment of any ancient city under Roman rule was tense. It has been estimated that more than 60 percent of the population of the Roman world was slaves. Tradition has it that Philemon took on a slave boy who was perhaps abandoned or left for dead. He named him Onesimus, which means "profitable," raised him in his own household, and treated him as a son. It is commonly thought that Onesimus received many privileges and opportunities. He was probably raised in a secure home and a warm church.

From the way Paul praises Philemon in the opening verses of the book, we can surmise that he was a committed Christian and servant to man and God. Paul describes him as a beloved friend and fellow laborer (v. 1), one who showed faith toward the Lord and love for the brethren (v. 5), one who shared his faith publicly (v. 6), and one who refreshed the brethren by caring for them (v. 7).

The Anatomy of Rebellion

Into this household of faith the spirit of rebellion dared to enter. Let us examine the anatomy of the rebellion of Onesimus.

First, it is obvious that this young man had never found the living Lord of his master. Instead he had only had "religion"—a set of rules and regulations, dos and don'ts.

As a speaker who has addressed millions of teens, I can assure you that religion can be cold and dead. What is needed is a red-hot, real religion, not rituals, not only resolutions, and not vain repetitions. What is needed is a relationship with the resurrected One.

Onesimus had head knowledge, but he had never had a heart change even though the church he was raised in was considered one of the most dynamic and balanced churches of the first century. Paul himself probably ministered there, as is implied in Colossians 4:9.

The life of piety and committed service to a warm church was shown daily to Onesimus, but this was not enough to change him. All that he saw was the surface of religion, and just below that was his rebellion. While he outwardly appeared to go along with Philemon, Onesimus stole from him and then ran away to a faroff country where he wasted his life, his money, and his future.

No doubt there were many sleepless nights back home, nights spent agonizing over mistakes made, words that were said, words that weren't said. Ah, the insight of hindsight. There must have been feelings of hopelessness and helplessness.

Enter Paul

As Onesimus continued to run, his path ran straight into the apostle Paul. God answered Philemon's prayers and arranged for Onesimus to be in Rome, where he was brought face to face with Paul. This is evident because Paul refers to Onesiumus as one "whom I have begotten while in my chains" (v. 10). As a prisoner Paul made a spiritual impact and impression on the rebel Onesimus.

I believe verse 15 may have been written just for waiting, praying parents. These words are like ointment to the wounded heart: "*Perhaps he departed for a while for this purpose, that you might receive him forever.*"

It is tempting for us to believe that sometimes we, or someone close to us, have so frustrated God's plan for our lives that we will never again be of much use to Him. "Man, I've done it now," or "I've had it with that boy," or "This is the last straw." But Paul gives us a different perspective. At the very least this verse tells us that those who depart for awhile can still return forever. Your child may have jumped ship, but rescue is still available.

In fact, the verse may be saying even more. Notice that Paul says that Onesimus departed for awhile *for a purpose*. In the grammar of the original language the first part of the sentence is closely connected to the last part. It is a purpose statement in which Paul may be suggesting that God may have even intended to use the "departing" for His glory. My own experience bears this out. Although I wasted six years behind the chemical curtains of alcohol and drugs, today I speak to millions attempting to recall them from the glitter of the "far country."

Keep the Porch Light On

Continue, dear parent, to pray that the temporary loss of your child will become an eternal gain. It is not uncommon for a parent who has been embarrassed or deeply hurt to close the door and prevent reconciliation. But Onesiumus' story tells us never to give up, to "keep the porch light on." Tough love longs for a second chance to have him back again.

The attitude of the father in the parable of the prodigal son should be our example. "But when he was still a great way off, his father saw him and had compassion, and ran and fell on his neck and kissed him" (Luke 15:20). Our attitude toward the child who is away must be one of an open door and a burning light.

In May 1991, while preaching in the concert hall in the Olympic Village in Moscow, I witnessed this principle in action. There was an overflow crowd and the atmosphere was electric. The contemporary Christian musical group Truth had performed an incredible concert, and I preached on the theme "Because He Lives."

As I gave an invitation, I stood in amazement as hundreds pressed their way to the front to make a profession of faith in Christ. Suddenly an elderly woman started screaming and running from one side of the auditorium to the other, weeping and shouting all the while. It was obvious something significant was taking place.

The interpreter soon explained, "This woman has been praying for forty years for her children. She had them baptized secretly as small children. Because of the iron-clad rule of Communism, her children had grown up atheists, members of the Communist party. And they are alcoholics."

But on this night of destiny, three of the woman's grown children and several grandchildren came forward to receive Christ. She was proclaiming, "God is faithful, my children have come home!" For more than forty years she made and sold candles at the Russian Orthodox Church since that was the only form of service allowed, and she continued to pray.

Waiting for the Return

Just as Philemon must have waited for Onesimus to return, I want to share a modern-day version of that story, one that shows how the Lord hears as parents pray for a good influence over their children even as they are running from home and from self. A loving mother gave me permission to share her story, and the names have been changed.

"Our son Richard left a Christian facility that we had hoped would be of help to him and another boy. Together they decided to hitchhike across the country to California, where the boy told him he could find a job. We were notified by the facility of his decision and waited for several days to hear from him.

"We were totally helpless; only God could be our strength and protection in his life. Yes, God once again intervened. We received a phone call from someone in Arizona saying they had found some luggage on the road with Richard's name and phone number.

"Immediately we remembered a family vacation in Arizona where Richard had met a girl. We looked in his room, found her telephone number, and called. The girl's dad told us that Richard had just called and would be calling back in thirty minutes to talk to his daughter. We asked him to ask Richard to call us immediately.

"When our son called he was in tears, saying he was scared, hungry, and had lost all his luggage. He was truly shocked when we told him that we had found his luggage and him through prayer and God's leading. There was never a doubt in my heart and mind that God was answering my prayer and that physical protection was over Richard, though he was having to learn some real hard lessons about life."

This mom shared with me some lessons she had learned through this ordeal that she would like to pass on to other parents:

- As much as it hurt, we soon learned that it had to be his idea to come home, just as the prodigal son "came to himself."

- Because of the intensity of the hurt, it is easy to give control of your heart and life to the rebellious one and allow him to play games with the family's emotions. The father waited at home and did not go after the son, but was ready to receive him at any time. In the meantime, he continued with his own life and the rest of the family.

- The embarrassment of an ungodly son cannot manipulate me into trying to cover up his sin. I cannot take it as a personal assassination of my parenting skills or my self-esteem. Others do not have to understand, as long as I believe I am doing what God has led me to do for this child.

- I must leave the line of communication open, and I must offer my love unconditionally, but I must never change my standards or give up a belief.

- I cannot allow my other family members to be traumatized by the stress of the one. The other children in the family should not have to pay for the mistakes of the prodigal child. By committing to pray together, you develop a bond with the other children and a hope that each can use to encourage the other as depression enters each individual in a cycle.

- I must not respond in anger, because by doing so I relieve him of the guilt of wrongdoing.

- I must pray and believe that, as he runs, he will run eventually into the arms of a Christian who will have an influence on his life, as in the case of Onesimus and Paul.

- The humility of his being arrested and spending time in jail cannot cause me to step in and relieve the consequence.

Reactions to Rebellion

The departure of a child to a far country commonly produces some reactions for which we need to be prepared. You may ask, "Who is this stranger living with me? He seems to love everything I hate—when he knows I hate it, he smiles as though he won. As he rebels, I get angry, and he is then relieved of the guilt because my response is now the focus instead of his behavior. He has tested every one of the beliefs that I hold dear in an effort to prove me inconsistent. He is hurt, and he dislikes himself, so he wants me to say that I dislike him, too, to prove his feelings about himself. In his deep hurt and pain, he acts as though he doesn't care about anything but reacting and rebelling against me."

During this time, take care of yourself and your other family relationships. One mother I met was obsessed with somehow trying to rescue her child. This can become a dissection of yourself to try to discover what went wrong, what the problem was, where you made a mistake. For the child's sake and for your own, you have to continue to live. You have to take some time for release and relaxation.

This obsession with vicariously living out the pain and disappointment of a child may cause a loss of the relationship with the other children. I hope you will make time for them as well as for releasing the stress you feel. I have long encouraged couples to have a date night for just the husband and wife during which the stresses and disappointments can be left behind. I would encourage you to go ahead with vacation plans and to give yourself permission to still enjoy life. Care for thyself.

Rescue Stories

The following story by a prodigal who returned is excerpted from a five-page letter sent to me by the daughter of a friend in the ministry, and is used by permission:

> My parents truly did a wonderful job of raising me. I believe they raised me to the best of their knowledge and brought me up in Christ, but I chose the opposite path to which they had no control. Although I accused them at times after I became rebellious, I know that they were only acting out of frustration and pain for me. At that point only God and my willingness could rescue me.
>
> I believe I allowed Satan to lure me in by a boy I dated for four years in high school. His parents sold drugs; he sold drugs and used them. I thought I could help him (now I know it was my gift of mercy); yet he hindered me. He was all the bad I had never known, and that intrigued me, yet it almost destroyed me.
>
> My parents tried to tell me. I am very strong-willed and always had the I'll-show-you attitude (which is now a positive).
>
> Even as my parents prayed, I continued to run. God chased me for a good two years, asking me to come back to my relationship with Him. The guilt drove me even further into drinking and partying. Then one night I had a dream and in it God spoke to me of His forgiveness, but I also had an understanding of His wrath.
>
> I went home that summer and told my parents I had to change my life and had to leave my friends and remove myself from my environment to do it. Months before, my mom and dad had surrendered my life to God's control in prayer.
>
> I am now married to a wonderful Christian man and work in a job where I talk with parents and teens daily who struggle with exactly what my family struggled with. Praise God that He follows after His own children, and longs for them to come home!

In other testimonies I have received, it was shared that associating with a rebellious crowd seemed "cool" and boosted self-esteem because the teen was allowed in. The more upset parents became, the more the child knew she was the center of the picture and could demand attention and energy. When this is allowed to happen, she wins and you lose.

There is great strength in rehearsing what God has already done in the life of your child and the good memories of the past. In *Prodigals and Those Who Love Them*, Ruth Bell Graham tells the story of many well-known prodigals and also shares some of her own private journaling during the long wait for her own prodigal sons. She gives the following helps to make the trial easier:

1. It helps when I know Who is in control.

2. It helps when I know I'm not alone in my suffering.

3. It helps when I know the purpose of God behind it (His glory, which is mentioned sixteen times in 1 Peter).

4. It helps because I become more compassionate with an understanding of others.

Ruth Graham used a wonderful Scripture that I had never seen and one that you may want to keep in your heart: "And there is hope in thine end, saith the Lord, that thy children shall come again to their own border" (Jer. 31:17 KJV).

When you have a prodigal child, remember: The final chapter has not yet been written.

16

Code Blue

How to Respond When the Going Gets Tough

The call "Code blue!" blasted through the intercom at the maternity ward. By some revelation, I knew the emergency alarm signaled trouble for my wife, even though moments earlier she had been vibrant and smiling, sending me to tell family and friends that the baby would be here very soon. Now she lay motionless as specialists worked feverishly to revive her.

Trained hands placed defibrillator paddles over Cindy's heart. Someone counted off seconds while the machine charged. I heard scraps of "Stand back!" A dull thud—the shock to Cindy's heart. Her body tightened, then flopped on the bed like a rag doll. At that moment something inside me silently left its dwelling place.

"She's dead, isn't she?" I asked.

"No, not yet," the doctor responded quietly. . . . "They're doing everything they can."[1]

This true story happened to one of my closest friends, Dr. Ike Reighard. I'll never forget his call to me that afternoon: "Jay, it's Ike. I've lost Cindy." Probably no other story I've heard describes as poignantly the sudden transition from a healthy, smiling person about to give birth to a person in need of immediate resuscitation.

"Code blue" is the terminology used in hospitals for a life-threatening emergency. Lights flash, hospital personnel scurry everywhere, equipment is rushed into place, and doctors are called in as every possible resource is mobilized to meet the patient's need in the moment of crisis.

Emergencies strike families, too. It is easy to raise kids when everything seems to be under control, but when a crisis occurs— it is "code blue" at your house! Such a state of emergency can hit a family suddenly and unexpectedly. Drugs . . . alcohol . . . arrest . . . pregnancy . . . they can all devastate a family without warning. (I would add that *any* addiction is a spiritual emergency.)

Fortunately, "code blue" doesn't have to mean sudden death. How a parent responds at these times of crisis will often determine the extent of the crisis itself. Some parents delay responding, hoping the problem will just go away. Others overreact in such a way that only makes the problem worse. But many parents act with courage and resourcefulness to minimize damage and promote healing.

The Code Blue Response

When a "code blue" crisis occurs in a hospital, specific procedures are followed, each of which has application to crisis times in the family:

1. Push the emergency button and get help. This has to happen as soon as the problem is discovered. The slightest delay can prove fatal. In hospitals, the nurse does not attempt to deal with the situation herself; she calls for someone with more expertise who will know just what everyone needs to do.

2. The whole team comes. While one person with special authority and skill is in charge, others must consider themselves called to the scene and commissioned to help. There must be enough personnel to fit the nature of the emergency.

3. The airway is cleared for breath. When it's really "code blue" at your house, you need to respond quickly and positively to the situation that is actually life threatening. Kids in a crisis are mainly dealing with the issue of survival. This is not the time to try to deal with all of the other issues in their lives. A girl who has been sexually assaulted isn't ready to hear a parental lecture about her driving habits.

4. Get the heart started. Once the airway is clear, the heart has to be bumped, sometimes in a shocking and violent manner. In a family emergency, the heart of each family member—that enduring energy which makes him or her tick—will be called on.

5. Unorthodox methods may be resorted to. Sometimes the situation is such that the usual techniques do not work. In these situations the team may do some very unusual things that would not be considered safe or orthodox for a normal patient. Such techniques as intervention and confrontation may be called for in family crises.

6. Accurate diagnosis is essential. Sometimes the team will have a good idea what led to the failure, especially if it concerns a patient who is already under care. But in each case it is vital to understand just what it was that shut down and led to the attack. Tests are run and interviews held to see what went wrong. The rule of thumb is, the longer the problem has lasted, the longer recovery will take. If we are dealing with a stabbing victim, the recovery will likely be short term; if it is a patient who has had chronic kidney or liver troubles, the recovery may take a long time. In the family, a long history of rebellion may take months to cure; failing a single class may heal more quickly.

7. The patient is then taken to ICU. This is invariable. The patient is never allowed simply to go home or back to a regular hospital bed. He must go to a place where his every move can be monitored until it is clear that he is out of immediate danger. This may vary from grounding to strict curfews to enrollment in a treatment center.

8. Regular monitoring is essential. After being released from intensive care, the patient is still monitored and checked regularly, either in his room or on an outpatient basis for as long as necessary. Don't think you can solve a family crisis by administering a single "dose" of medicine and then leave the patient on his own.

9. Followup assessment must be made. Whether in the hospital or at home, it is necessary to discover how this all transpired. "Before" and "after" descriptions must be made in order to alert everyone to the danger signs that may signal a future recurrence of the problem.

Dr. Ed Hindson, vice-president of Missouri Baptist College, conducts family life conferences in which he helps parents perceive whether events in a child's life call for a "code blue" response. Before a crisis hits, we are in a state of equilibrium (or balance):

Normal Pressures of Life

Emotional Balance

1. Able to cope
2. Finds support from family and friends
3. Deals with problems effectively
4. Maintains emotional balance

In this chart, the individual is under pressure, but he is able to handle the pressure and navigate through life. By contrast, a crisis situation is indicated when the chart changes thus:

Crisis Situation

Emotional Imbalance

1. Unable to cope
2. Lack of support
3. Lashes out at problems
4. Loses emotional balance

The Minirth-Meier psychiatric organization has prepared the following helpful checklist.

Signs and Signals of Troubled Kids

- Deterioration of grades
- Chronic truancy
- Chronic school failure
- Interest in the occult
- Mood swings
- General apathy
- Drug/alcohol use
- Blatant sexual behavior
- Verbal or physical displays
- Withdrawal/feeling of hopelessness
- Family history of substance abuse or mental illness
- Extreme change in appearance or friends
- Inability to cope with routine matters/relationships
- Sleeplessness, fatigue
- Low self-esteem
- Sadness, crying
- Secretive
- Suicidal thoughts
- Unexplained accidents
- Death of significant person
- Poor impulse control

What Can a Parent Do?

A parent in a crisis situation who loses his or her sense of emotional balance will only precipitate a more severe crisis. For example, a teenager who admits he has been on drugs is really crying out for help. But if the parent goes all to pieces and begins verbally attacking the teenager, he will likely say to himself, "That's the last time I'm going to get honest about my struggles."

Overreacting parents often drive kids into an emotional shell from which they are reluctant to venture. *Underreacting* parents send a message to their kids that says, "I just don't care." Either response can be devastating when the individual loses his emotional balance.

Let me make several simple suggestions for steps of action when it is "code blue" at your house:

1. Don't panic. This is no time to lose control of yourself. You will only add confusion to the crisis. Screaming, hollering, or making demands will not fix what has gone wrong. Remember, God is still in control, despite the crisis. He knows what you need to do.

2. Act quickly. Some well-thought-out action is necessary. Don't just sit there hoping the problem will solve itself or just go away. *Timing* is crucial in a crisis.

3. Seek advice. Don't hesitate to seek the advice of knowledgeable people: pastors, counselors, teachers, lawyers, police, and other officials. Remember, these people are not the "enemy." They are there to help you. Don't try to solve the crisis alone. Seek the advice of those who can really help.

4. Stick to the main issues. While your teenager may have several areas in which he needs improvement (e.g., self-acceptance, personal discipline, study habits, etc.), it is important to stick with the major issues of the crisis until they are resolved. Only when the crisis subsides will the teenager be clearheaded enough to focus on the other issues in his life.

5. Balance love and discipline. At the same time, you will need to balance love with discipline when necessary so that your teenager doesn't just run over you.

The Crisis of Suicide

No "code blue" situation is more urgent than tendencies toward self-destruction. Of course this, too, is rooted in sin, for sin is always self-destructive. It may soon lead to depression and then even to thoughts of suicide.

When a teenager has experimented extensively with sin, he will often develop the attitude, "I've tried everything there is to try. I might have done everything there is to do, and I'm not happy! I might as well be dead!"

Suicide is one of the leading causes of death among America's teenagers. Thousands of young people take their lives every year because they come to the end of their emotional "rope" and decide that life is not worth living. When a teen believes his family and friends do not have the answer to real meaning and purpose in life, he may give up on life itself.

This tragedy need not ever take place in your family. You can forestall it by recognizing that your teenager's problems are very real and must be dealt with as such. You must also recognize that these problems began, in most cases, at home and that you are as much a part of the problem as you are a part of the solution.

Young people may consider suicide for a variety of reasons:

Inescapable problems. A sense of hopelessness prevails because there seems to be no way out (for example, family problems, social relationships, loss of job, poor school grades).

To "get even." Because feelings have been hurt, the offended may use suicide to lash out in vengeance, hoping to make the offending survivors feel guilty.

To gain attention. Suicide is a cry for attention. The teen may hope that he fails in his attempt and that he will earn lavish attention afterward.

To join deceased loved ones. This is particularly true when a mother, father, or mate has passed away.

To avoid consequences. This can involve financial indebtedness, punishment for commission of a crime, or an illegitimate pregnancy.

To pledge love. In the case of a broken relationship, one that is either forced by parents or by one of the partners, suicide can be a statement of "I can't live without you"—a playback of the Romeo and Juliet story.

17

Special Settings

Blended and Single Families

While crises can occur in any family, some settings deserve special attention and extra measures of prevention.

The Blended Family

With so many new divorces in America today (over a million a year), there are now a record number of remarriages. While most second marriages are begun with high hopes, many of them collapse because of the unique problems faced by blended families.

Many psychologists believe that it takes three to seven years for blended families to really blend with each other. Kids are can threatened by the mixing of two families. Issues such as space, privacy, ownership, and discipline can threaten the stability of the blended family. The older the children are when the remarriage occurs, the more resistant they usually are to the new parental figure whom they may view as an intruder.

Even in Christian families, remarriage poses special challenges and problems. Some people assume that if their first partner was not a believer, marrying a Christian will automatically mean their new family will work fine. But this is often not the case. Just because a person is a professing Christian doesn't necessarily mean he or she is an ideal marriage partner or parent.

One frustrated wife told me that blended families aren't the "Brady Bunch." "It just isn't that simple," she explained. It takes time, patience, and often forgiveness to learn to accept each other, and each other's children.

"It doesn't happen easily, but it does work," one husband told me. "But it only works because we are willing to work at it," he added.

Here are some suggestions for forestalling "code blue" situations in a blended family.

1. Don't assume the kids are happy. Children are vulnerable to the pressures of divorce and remarriage and the trauma of having lost a parent in death. At times they may appear to be doing fine. At other times they will obviously be struggling. Be patient with them. Listen to them. Don't lecture them about how lucky they should feel to have you in their lives. You must end their hurt. Just because you married their mom doesn't make you their dad.

2. Keep communication open. Initially, the new husband and wife are absorbed with each other. They want to have an extended honeymoon. But the kids will soon be asking for your attention. Don't argue. Talk, listen, think, and pray together.

3. Don't blame each other's kids. One of the greatest problems for blended families is the "your kids" versus "my kids" mentality. Don't take sides. Don't pit the kids against each other, and don't let the kids pit you and your partner against each other.

Put yourself in the children's shoes. Teenagers in a blended family need time to adjust. They want to be loved, accepted, and understood. Whether teenagers show it or not, they usually enter the new family with doubts, fears, and insecurities. They need an overabundance of love and assurance from both of you.

Single Parents and Teenagers

With a million new divorces each year since 1975 and a national divorce rate of nearly 50 percent, the issue of single parenting is going to have to be faced more and more by the church. In fact the family must be redefined to include both single-parent homes and childless couples.

Single parents' relationship with their teens may be damaged by feelings of inadequacy, or even that they aren't a "real family." While single parents cannot be both a father and mother, they can fulfill the responsibility that God has given them. A widowed or divorced mother can be a complete mother to her children. She can be a fulfilled and creative woman who sets a godly example of spiritual influence for her family. A single father can be a great motivator and encourager as much as a married father.

Single parents' parenting may be complicated by grief and guilt. Heartbroken husbands and wives have often come to me explaining their traumatic experiences over the loss of a marriage partner who refused to reconcile with them and divorced them against their wishes. These people already feel a great sense of misery and failure. We certainly cannot minister to them if we treat them as spiritual castoffs and further reinforce their sense of failure. Prejudice in this matter has caused some Christian workers to fail to give any help at all to people who are in great need of help. Remember, it was Jesus Himself who said, "Those who are well have no need of a physician, but those who are sick" (Matt. 9:12).

Let me emphasize that you do not have to become the victim of someone else's sin. "But you don't understand," you say, "he left me." Your husband (or wife) may have sinned against you and hurt you deeply, but you still don't have to let your life be ruined by another person's sin.

God is the author of marriage, not divorce. He is against divorce (Matt. 5:31–32). But *He is not against the divorced person.* The Scripture clearly states that the divorcer (not the divorced) is responsible for breaking up the marriage. Perhaps in your case you wrongly divorced your partner before your conversion. While divorce is permanent and imposes limitations, it is still forgivable. There is only one "unpardonable sin" (blasphemy against the Holy Spirit), and it is not divorce!

Stop blaming yourself for something you cannot change. Here are a list of don'ts for single parents.

1. Don't blame God for your circumstances (divorced or widowed).

2. Don't criticize your divorced partner in front of your children. Remember, he or she is still their parent also.

3. Don't condemn yourself for circumstances beyond your control—"I wish I had done better"; "If I had said this, maybe he would not have left"; "If I had only been there, maybe he would not have died."

4. Don't wish you were someone else. That is irresponsibly avoiding reality. Such "daydreaming" will ruin your kids.

5. Don't speculate endlessly about what might have been. The time has come to fully accept things as they are now. If your partner left and remarried, the Scripture advises not to take him back (see Deut. 24:1–4).

6. Don't overly "spiritualize" your problems. Your kids will see right through all that drippy talk about how you are really satisfied things worked out the way they did. Don't misquote Romans 8:28 and just pretend that you feel that things have worked out for the best.

7. Don't excuse yourself. It takes two to tango. Don't put all the blame on your former partner.

8. Don't become overly dependent on the wrong people. Don't constantly run to others with your problems. It will confuse you. Learn to place your greatest dependence on the Lord Himself.

9. Don't dominate your kids in the hope that they won't turn out like you. You may drive them off by being too much of a "martyr."

10. Don't worry about the future; trust God to guide you.

11. Emphasize your possibilities, not your problems. Rather than being defeated by your situation, concentrate on what you can do effectively. There is much good that you can still accomplish. If you are a woman, be the best mom you can be to your kids—don't try to be a dad to them. If you are a man, be the best dad you can to

your kids—don't try to be their mom. Be yourself! Your
own honesty, sincerity, and integrity will mean more to
your children than anything else.

God's grace provides forgiveness and redemption for our sins,
and He can also redeem seemingly hopeless family situations. He
who loved us so much can enable us to show His love and forgiveness as well. God did not save you in order to make you miserable.
Despite your personal struggles with single parenting or blended
families, God's grace is still sufficient for your needs.

Whatever you may feel is lacking in your family situation, it
is not a lack of God's love or grace. Both are freely available to all
who will receive them. You may not be able to change the *past*,
but you can change the *present*, and that will change the *future*.

God still has great things in store for your family. Living by
His principles and with faith in His provisions, you can face tomorrow with confidence. Remember, God is there in your moment of need. He is ultimately in control of your life. He loves you
deeply, so much that there is nothing you can do to make Him
love you more or love you less. Living with that assurance will
help you face the future now.

Christian parents, God has granted us stewardship over a
precious commodity. Let us thank Him for that. In fact, I
would encourage you to stop right now, lay this book down for
a moment, and breathe a prayer of gratitude to the Almighty
Lord for the honor He has given you by entrusting you with
your children.

After praying, let us agree together that we are going to be
God's parents to those kids. No matter what struggles there have
been, no matter how many times we have failed, no matter where
they may be in their spiritual pilgrimage, they are still our kids and
we can still make an impact on their lives.

Do you have a good kid gone bad?

Remember: God has had problems with His kids, too, and
He hasn't given up yet! Neither should you. Let us remind ourselves of several triumphant truths found in Scripture:

1. With God all things are possible (Matt. 19:26).

2. The final chapter has not been written on your child, as long as he is still living.

3. If we possess a living faith, then we should remain confident that the best is yet to come.

In Genesis 31:49, Laban and Jacob made a covenant together: The Lord watch between me and thee, while we are absent one from another. The Hebrew word for *watch* in this passage has several implications. It denotes something that is bright and shining—as brilliant as the Lord who would one day come as the light of the world, who watches over His own. The word implies a watching for danger at a great distance and the willingness to warn others if danger is discovered.[2]

During these days when understanding may seem dark and confidence may be dim, remember to leave the porch light on and to watch.

APPENDIX 1

STAGES OF ADOLESCENCE*

The chart on the following two pages depicts the life changes that an adolescent experiences.

*By Paul Warren, M.D., Minirth-Meier Clinic, Richardson, Texas. Used by permission.

Type of Change	Early Adolescence Ages 11–13 Grades 5–7	Middle Adolescence Ages 14–16 Grades 8–10	Late Adolescence Ages 17–25+ Grades 11+
Physical	Puberty begins, rapid change in height, particularly for girls	Continued rapid growth, especially for boys. Puberty ends around 16.	Puberty completed.
Communication	Often poor and sparse. Seem to lose or refuse to use verbal abilities.	Practice extremes "all or nothing at all." Suddenly switch from one extreme to the other.	Can converse, using give and take, on a variety of subjects.
Separation and Individuation	Primary identification changes from parents to peers, as a group, not as individuals. Other significant adults also important.	Still identify more with peers, but now as individuals, although this fluctuates. Autonomy (dependence on self) begins.	Establish more autonomy but with some attachment to other significant peers and adults. Growing ability for intimacy.
Morals	Begin questioning family morals, as they discover parents aren't perfect.	Further questioning and even rejecting of family and societal standards.	Restructuring of standards of their own, usually very similar to parents'.
Behaviors	Disorganized, ambivalent, self-centered, easily bored. Fearful of maturing with self-doubts. Outwardly act fearless and overly self-assured.	Experiment with new fluctuating behaviors. See self as performer watched by world that sees only faults, so idealize self as unique, not bound by natural laws. ("Bad things —drug reactions—can't happen to me!") Want to experience extreme highs and lows— sad and happy songs, or even through drugs.	Begin responsible behaviors, temper idealism with reality, practice more long-term planning. See life as series of highs and lows, not isolated incidents.

Identity	Tend to see self as all good or all bad.	View of self fluctuates. Learning how to be average.	See self as human, both good and bad.
Sexuality	Have "crushes" and group interest in other sex. Males want a physical relationship, females a romantic one.	Experimenting with relationships, frequently in pairs. More interested in receiving than giving.	Developing ability for intimacy.
Career	Sublimate new sexual feelings into career choices—truck driver, cheerleader, etc.	Experiment with types of work. Learn what earning power is like, learn one-on-one responsibility to adults other than parents.	Narrow career goals and make final decision.
View of Parents	Discover and grieve that parents aren't perfect.	See parents as very imperfect, even stupid.	"Forgive" parents for imperfection, as own imperfection is recognized.

APPENDIX 2

YOUTH SURVEY FORM

1. How do you rate your relationship with your family? (10 = highest)

   10   9   8   7   6   5   4   3   2   1

   Do you spend a lot of time with your family?

   10   9   8   7   6   5   4   3   2   1

2. Are your parents active in church?   ☐ Yes   ☐ No

3. Has there been a divorce in your family?   ☐ Yes   ☐ No

4. What would you change about your family if you could?

   _____

   _____

   Why? _____

5. What are your greatest temptations to sin? List two.

   _____

6. Why do you think "good" kids do bad things?

   1. _____   2. _____

   3. _____   4. _____

   5. _____   6. _____

GOOD KIDS WHO DO BAD THINGS

7. What helps you to stay strong in your faith? ☐ Family?
   ☐ Church activities? ☐ Friends? ☐ Other?

8. Who is the most helpful to you in planning your life and help-
   ing you through stressful decisions? Number according to de-
   gree of influence: 5 being the most influential, and 1 the least
   influential.
   ☐ Parents
   ☐ Friends
   ☐ Other family
   ☐ School
   ☐ Church
   ☐ Other (Who? _____)

9. How does your relationship with your brother/sister affect your
   attitude about life?

10. How often do you feel depressed? (Circle one:)

            Rarely   Occasionally   Daily

    What do you think causes your depression?

11. How do you think depression affects the way you feel about
    yourself?_____

    _____

12. What makes you feel good about yourself?_____

    _____

    What makes you feel bad about yourself?_____ _

    _____

*If you have a personal testimony that you would like to share with us, you
may do so on the back of this sheet. What you share will be kept in total confidence, unless you express that you would like it shared with others struggling
with similar situations.*

Notes

Chapter 1—What Is a Good Kid?

1. Elizabeth Elliot, "Amy Carmichael," in *Heroes*, ed. Ann Spangler and Charles Turner (Ann Arbor, Mich.: Servant, 1990).

Chapter 2—The Lion's Roar

1. Tim LaHaye, *Sex Education Is for the Family* (Grand Rapids, Mich.: Zondervan, 1991).
2. *USA Today*, 19 May 1992.
3. Ibid.
4. Benjamin Spock, *Baby and Child Care* (New York: Pocket Books, 1957).
5. Robert S. McGee, "Preventing Substance Abuse," *Rapha Insights*, vol. 1, no. 13.
6. Emily Yoffe, "Girls Who Go Too Far," *Newsweek*, 22 July 1991, 58–59.
7. J. Allan Peterson, *The Myth of the Greener Grass* (Wheaton, Ill.: Tyndale, 1983), 89.

Chapter 3—Beyond the Glitter

1. George Barna, *The Frog in the Kettle* (Ventura, Calif.: Regal Books, 1990).
2. Quentin Schultze et al., *Dancing in the Dark* (Grand Rapids, Mich.: Eerdmans, 1991), 236. The criteria for movie making the authors refer to were originally part of a 1965 article in *Life* magazine.
3. Ibid.
4. Ibid., 247.

Chapter 4—Fasten Your Seatbelts

1. "Proverbs," *Commentary on the Old Testament*, vol. 2 (Grand Rapids, Mich.: Eerdmans, n.d.), 86–87.

2. From alumni birthday cards of Bill Gothard's Institute in Basic Life Principles, Oak Brook, Ill.
3. William Barclay, 1 Peter and James, The Daily Study Bible (New York: Westminster Press, 1969).
4. Ibid.
5. Ibid.
6. Kenneth Cooper, M.D., The Aerobics Program for Total Well-Being (New York: Bantam Books, 1982).
7. Kathy Koob, in Heroes, ed. Ann Spangler and Charles Turner (Ann Arbor, Mich.: Servant, 1990).
8. In Leading a Child to Independence (San Bernardino, Calif.: Here's Life Publishers, 1986).

Chapter 5—How Do You Spell Problems?

1. Ron Taffel, Parenting by Heart (Reading, Mass.: Addison-Wesley, 1991).
2. American Demographics, October 1991, 9–10.
3. Paul Meier, Christian Child-Rearing and Personality Development (Grand Rapids, Mich.: Baker, 1977).
4. Jet (June 1990): 64–65.
5. Bonaro Overstreet, Understanding Fear in Ourselves and Others (New York: Harper Brothers, 1951).

Chapter 7—A Matter of Heartitude

1. From "The Power of a Woman's Heart," unpublished manuscript by Diane Strack.

Chapter 8—I'll Climb with You

1. Howard Chua, "Going, Going . . . ," Time, 19 August 1991, 36.
2. Dorothy Corkhill Briggs, Your Child's Self-Esteem (New York: Doubleday, 1970).
3. Ken Blanchard, The One-Minute Manager (New York: William Morrow, 1981).
4. Zig Ziglar, Raising Positive Kids in a Negative World (Nashville, Tenn.: Oliver Nelson, 1985).

Chapter 9—A Taste of Heaven

1. Steven Covey, *The Seven Habits of Highly Effective People* (New York: Simon & Schuster, 1989).
2. Charles Stanley, *How to Keep Your Kids on Your Team* (Nashville, Tenn.: Oliver Nelson, 1986).
3. Catherine Marshall, *Meeting God at Every Turn* (New York: Bantam Books, 1980), 42.
4. Charles Hummel, *The Tyranny of the Urgent* (Downers Grove, Ill.: InterVarsity Press, 1980).

Chapter 10—Breaking the Cycle of Pain

1. Dusko Doder and Louise Branson, *Gorbachev: Heretic in the Kremlin* (New York: Viking Press, 1990).

Chapter 11—Friendly Fire

1. "Are American Workers Wimps?" *Inc.* (January 1992).

Chapter 12—Reaching for the Stars

1. W. Phillip Keller, "Otto C. Keller," in *Heroes*, ed. Ann Spangler and Charles Turner (Ann Arbor, Mich.: Servant, 1990), 269–84.
2. Ibid., 284.
3. Martin Seligman, *Learned Optimism* (New York: Random House, 1990), 13.
4. John Maxwell, *Be All You Can Be* (Wheaton, Ill.: Victor Books, 1987).
5. R. C. Sproul, "Thomas Aquinas," in *Heroes*, 258.
6. Ron Taffel, *Parenting by Heart* (Reading, Mass.: Addison-Wesley, 1991), 71.
7. McGee and McCallister, *Search for Significance*.
8. Paul Tournier, *The Whole Person in a Broken World* (New York: Harper & Row, 1963).

Chapter 13—Get Out the Big Guns

1. Wayne Biddle, "The Untold Story of the Patriot," *Discover* (June 1991): 74–78.

2. For a good guide to what your children should be learning educationally, see the various books by E. D. Hirsch, e.g., *Cultural Literacy*, *What Your First Grader Should Know*, *What Your Second Grader Should Know*, etc.

Chapter 14—Tearing Down the Chemical Curtain

1. "Straight Talk," a secular school presentation on values in the modern world by Jay Strack.
2. Cheryl Tevis, "Rural Health," *Successful Farming* (June 1991): 8.
3. *Journal of the American Medical Association*, 16 May 1990, 2282.

Chapter 16—Code Blue

1. Adapted from Ike Reighard, *Treasures from the Dark* (Nashville, Tenn.: Thomas Nelson, 1990) and used by permission.
2. Al Novak, *Hebrew Honey* (Houston: J. Countryman, 1987), 268.